AGING
IS NOT OPTIONAL:
HOW WE HANDLE IT — IS

A MANUAL FOR THE GREATEST JOURNEY
YOU WILL EVER MAKE

Ronald Higdon

Energion Publications
Gonzalez, Florida
2019

Cover Design: Henry Neufeld

ISBN13: 978-1-63199-704-4
Library of Congress Control Number: 2019909730

Energion Publications
P. O. Box 841
Gonzalez, FL 32560
850-525-3916

energion.com
pubs@energion.com

DEDICATION

*Dedicated to the countless senior adults who have
shared their stories and amazed me with their
depth of courage, faith, perception, and wisdom.*

TABLE OF CONTENTS

Preface

Things You Have the Right to Know

It is always helpful for me to know why the author wrote the book, what its intended purpose is, and the qualifications the writer brings to the subject. Simply being one of whom I am speaking (I am now in my mid eighties), is at least a beginning qualification. Being in pastoral ministry for over sixty years brought me into contact with senior adults on a continuing basis. Although I do not downplay in any way the formal education I received in college and seminary, there was so much yet to learn "in the field" which no classroom (or even textbook) was able to provide. At residences, nursing homes (assisted-care facilities), hospitals, intensive-care units, funeral homes, and cemeteries I came into contact with the elderly, their families, and friends. I heard the stories, the joys and sorrows, the concerns, the questions, and the words that came from deep within the hearts and souls of those who were facing the greatest issues life has to offer. I also spent almost two years doing basic research and assembling a list of what I consider to be some of the best resources available.

In a youth-oriented culture where old age is almost regarded as the unpardonable sin, there is not much space in our daily lives for the discussion of the one reality that is inescapable – aging. Scarlett O'Hara is not the only one who has ever said, "I'll think about that tomorrow. If I think about that today, I'll go crazy." My purpose in writing this book is to bring the good news that discussions about aging can bring new purpose, meaning, and hope to all of life – regardless of your present age. This is a book filled with perspectives and suggestions that can make the advancing years truly golden in the sense of satisfaction, meaning, and fulfillment. My prayer is that you will allow me to take you on the journey through this book and let me know if it was worth the trip. I believe you will be surprised at the number of discoveries and new insights you will find, discoveries and insights that will enlighten and enliven all of the remaining days of your life.

DOES IT ALWAYS HAVE TO BE THIS WAY?

In workshops, I have used the following quote and asked if the participants could guess who wrote these words:

> I never thought I would live to be this old. All my life I was taught how to die as a Christian, but no one ever taught me how I ought to live before I die. I wish they had because I am an old man now, and believe me, it's not easy.
>
> Growing old has been the greatest surprise of my life.[1]

No one *ever* gave me the correct answer: Billy Graham. Those lines come from his book *Nearing Home* which he wrote as he was approaching his 93rd birthday. A vast number of seniors over the years have echoed the surprise that came to Graham. I have never met anyone who "planned" on being old. Perhaps that is due to the four-myths, in various forms and in varying degrees, that one writer maintains continue to prevail in our culture: the myth of the super-centenarian, the myth of Shangri-La, the myth of Methuselah, and the Myth of the Fountain of Youth.[2]

> Your quality of life in old age will be the accumulation of the habits, beliefs, experiences and attitudes you've collected as you go through life. As you know, you won't suddenly arrive at old age. It will be merely an extension of

---

1   Graham, Billy. *Nearing Home* (Nashville: Thomas Nelson, 2011) vii, 1.
2   Fries, James F. and Lawrence M. Crapo, *Vitality and Again* (San Francisco: W. H. Freeman and Company, 1981), 11.

who you are now, what happens to you along the way, and whatever changes you make to improve your life.[3]

Although growth and change are always possible, I don't believe that one suddenly becomes something in old age that has never been present in life before. We only become more of what we have always been. That is why it is so important to concentrate on who we are throughout all of life. One woman confesses: "I thought I was prepared for my senior years.... I'd devoted a great deal of attention to being certain I'd be financially secure. But now I'm realizing I'm totally unprepared for the emotional and spiritual challenges I'm facing." [4] Much in this book will focus on the emotional and spiritual dimensions of our existence as human beings.

THE MOST IMPORTANT RESOURCE FOR AGING

"To know how to grow old is the master-work of wisdom, and one of the most difficult chapters in the great art of living" (Henri Frederic Amiel).[5] That master-work of wisdom rests with each individual and I trust that the book you are holding in your hands will contribute to a part of that wisdom. It has been said by many but none more plainly and clearly than in this simple sentence: "You are the most important resource for making your life work."[6]

PLEASE DON'T LET THIS BE A RED FLAG FOR YOU

In the course of this book you will find many references with varying points of view from a wide variety of authors. I do not doubt that some will surprise you but I trust that none will shock you. My education included advice which I have never forgotten:

---

3   Creagan, Edward T., Ed., *Mayo Clinic on Healthy Aging* (Rochester: Mayo Clinic, 2001), 8, 14.
4   Graham, Billy. *Nearing Home*, 23, 153.
5   Peck, M. Scott. *An Anthology of Wisdom* (Kansas City: Ariel Books, 1996), 278.
6   McGraw, Phillip C. *Life Strategies* (New York: Hyperion, 1999), 182.

"Let your reading and your research always include points of view different from your own and writers who come from entirely different orientations." Especially as we age, our knowledge needs to have greater width as well as depth that engender greater compassion and understanding. This does not mean that I have abandoned my commitment as a Christian minister and educator or that I am constantly revising what I believe. I simply bite my tongue when someone tells me, "I only listen to commentators who will underscore what I already believe and only read that which confirms my convictions." For me, that attitude produces a very small world and a very small mind, neither of which I maintain is helpful in the process of "successful" aging.

A CALL TO REPENTANCE

This, in truth, is the essence of this book but the word "repentance" needs some clarification. It has little to do with the common assumptions of regret, sorrow, and making up in some way for mistakes. The biblical word is *metanoia* and means "a new basic attitude, a different scale of values, a radical freethinking and returning (also involves new motivations)."[7] It calls for a new perspective, a new way of looking at things. (Repentance in the New Testament is a call to put on Kingdom glasses and see the world from an entirely different frame of reference.)

In the following pages we will explore various aspects of that new perspective and I will be asking you to put on the glasses of personal responsibility, hope, courage, faith, and determination to live each and every day fully and richly. This always involves hard work and a refusal to ignore either the realities of existence or of the possibilities that come each day if we only have the eyes to see and the ears to listen.

---

7   Kung, Hans. *The Christian Challenge* (Garden City: Doubleday, 1979), 278.

The Introduction pleads the case for making Reality 101 the basic required course for any interaction with life. My older son had a plaque in his office that read: *IT IS WHAT IT IS.* The beginning of any decision to deal with a situation is the recognition of all the factors involved. This is not negative thinking but the realization that how I deal with any of life's circumstances has to begin with an honest evaluation of what I am facing.

Chapter 1 discusses facing the biggest of these realities: the losses and limitations that seem to come in increasing quantities. Our ability to deal with the losses and limitations that come throughout all of life is the best preparation for constructively dealing with the often extreme number that assault us in our later years.

Chapter 2 has already been suggested in the Preface as being basic to everything in this book. It is not what happens to us in life, it is how we respond that makes all the difference in the world. It is our perspective, our attitude, and our reflection on the meaning of our experience that determine the steps we will take and the outcomes that will result.

Chapter 3 asks the question about those automatic perspectives and assumptions that form our default setting on practically all of life's issues. We will examine many of the aspects of these settings and how to consciously re-examine them in order to ascertain their validity.

Chapter 4 asks one of the basic questions of life and faith: Do we aim for control or guidance? Even though it is obvious we have far less control over practically anything than we like to acknowledge, this chapter suggests the major differences between the two approaches and the needed balance.

Chapter 5 reflects on the major ingredient of laughter (a sense of humor) that takes its title from the recommendation: *Take two laughs and call me in the morning.* This is not intended as a prescription of how to laugh your way out of everything but maintains that laughter can be very therapeutic and a necessary ingredient in a healthy emotional life.

Chapter 6 always comes up as one of the four major ingredients in successful aging: having meaning and purpose in your life. There will be many pleasant surprises in this chapter about the ways and the places these can be found.

Chapter 7 takes an advertising slogan of years ago from Coca Cola and expands it into the demand for reflection and contemplation. It is not only the pause that refreshes, it is the pause that sets the stage for whatever the day has to offer.

Chapter 8 presents the challenge of living gratefully, generously, and discovering ways to celebrate something (or, at least, many things) every day. I give two of the best and surprising examples of this I have ever known. I think you will find the story delightful and inspiring.

Chapter 9, exercising your body and your mind, is emphasized in every study on aging I have ever read. We discuss the benefits and the ways to do both without being overwhelmed by either.

Chapter 10 faces head-on the worst fear that most seniors have: Alzheimer's. While not sidestepping the tragedy of the illness, you will find many suggestions for those who begin experiencing dementia as well as helpful resources for caregivers.

Chapter 11 combines Paul's hopeful words about *inwardly being renewed day by day* with the conversation that never stops – the one we have with ourselves. How to monitor this conversation has much to do with just how much renewal we experience.

Chapter 12 is the call to continue developing the unique person you are. Our culture too often defaults to identifying individuals with the aging group to which they belong: "Oh, you know how teenagers are;" "Those young adults are just the 'me' generation;" "Old people are just like that." The biblical teaching is that each of us has been created in the image of God and are unique human beings unlike anyone else in the world. This chapter lays out the challenge and the possibilities to continue the greatest adventure life presents us: continuing to become all that God has placed within us.

Chapter 13 is perhaps one of the most difficult for many of us – remaining proactive in our later years and asking the question each day, "Who is responsible for my life?" Being proactive means I give up the status of victim in large part by recognizing that I am responsible for my life – period.

Chapter 14 is what I have been talking about for over sixty years: how to tap the resources of faith and hope, especially in times when faith seems to have lost its reason for being and things seem hopeless beyond repair. This chapter is a journey of real faith in a real world with some real hope.

Chapter 15 is one which is basic in any book on "spirituality" I have ever read. It is usually described in terms of mastering the art of letting go. I have called it learning how to negotiate effectively the endings and beginnings that are a part of all our lives – even in the earlier years.

Chapter 16 is perhaps one the best known tenants of almost every major religion in the world: live in the now. Living in the present moment seems so obvious because it is the only time we have in which we can live, but many seem to continue to find it extremely difficult. In this section we will hear the command: "Get off the regret express; it isn't going anywhere."

The Conclusion, *Bringing it All Together,* is more than a summary of the material. It gives me the opportunity to highlight what I have said in the chapters but it is also my opportunity to think out loud about what has occurred to me in the writing of this book and also to introduce some new writers and resources.

THE STRUCTURE OF THIS BOOK

We will be examining 16 basic areas to which we need to give attention as we age. Each chapter begins with *Setting the Stage,* consisting of quotations that, hopefully, begin the process of analyzing and reflecting on the material that follows. Each section concludes with *Questions for Reflection, Discovery, and Conversation.* My prayer is that this book will help change aging from a problem to be solved into an adventure into a new dimension of living.

QUESTIONS FOR REFLECTION, DISCOVERY, AND CONVERSATION

1. Did Billy Graham's statement about the surprise of old age surprise you?
2. Do you think most of us are prepared emotionally and spiritually for our senior years?
3. Which chapters are you most anxious to read? Which would you prefer to skip?

Introduction

A Reality Check

Setting the Stage

While aging is inevitable, how you will age is often largely up to you. Aging invites you to have discernment.[8]

In 2016 the Oxford Dictionaries announced that "after much discussion, debate, and research," post-truth was the Word of the Year, as an adjective defined as "relating to or denoting circumstances in which objective facts are less influential in shaping public opinion than appeals to emotion and personal belief."[9]

The real is hard, time-consuming, and badly lit. I much prefer fantasy.[10]

Despite tempting claims, no product has been proved to prevent or reverse aging.[11]

"Just the Facts...Just the Facts"

A popular radio and TV show of another time, *Dragnet*, used this classic line whenever the detectives were attempting to get in-

---

8   Wolfelt, Alan D. & Kirby J. Duvall, *Healing Your Grief About Aging* (Fort Collins, CO: Companion Press, 2012), 4.

9   Evans, Harold *Do I Make Myself Clear?* (New York: Little, Brown and Company, 2017), 194.

10 Lamott, Anne *Hallelujah Anyway* (New York: Riverhead Books, 2017), 136.

11 Creagan, Edward T. ed., *Mayo Clinic On Healthy Aging*, 48.

formation about a situation. They were asking for the basics about a situation unclouded by interpretation or perspectives of any kind. In our present world of social media, bloggers, talk-shows, and personal opinion columns, this kind of fact-finding is extremely difficult to come by. Some have gone so far as to conclude that "there are no facts, only perceptions." Well, yes and no. Gravity is a fact; my perception to the contrary will only have disastrous results.

When someone says, "It seems to me…", I always want to inquire, "Based on what?" A popular book of some years ago in its title and first page promised far too much and made me skeptical about its contents. (Preliminary note: the author doesn't mean these things literally). The author is Deepak Chopra and the book's title is *Ageless Body, Timeless Mind: The Quantum Alternative to Growing Old.* Part one promises to bring us to the land where no one is old.

> We will explore a place where the rules of everyday ex-istence do not apply. These rules explicitly state that to grow old, become frail, and die is the ultimate destiny of all.…I want to suspend your assumptions about what we call reality so that we can become pioneers in a land where youth, vigor, renewal, creativity, joy, fulfillment, and timelessness are the common experience of everyday life, where old age, senility, infirmity, and death do not exist and are not even entertained as a possibility.[12]

In all fairness to the author, there are many helpful suggestions offered that do not rely on the elimination of the realities of aging and dying. My decades of ministry to persons who were aging belie the interpretation of the exaggerations of the above claims as facts. This is a fact: "While we have been remarkably successful at delaying death, crucially, we have failed to delay aging."[13]

---

12   Chopra, Deepak. *Ageless Body, Timeless Mind* (New York: Harmony Books, 1993), 1, 3.

13   Brown, Guy. *The Living End* (London: Macmillan, 2008), 5.

Happiology Continues to be as Popular as Ever

"Put on a Happy Face," "Let a Smile Be Your Umbrella," and "Accentuate the Positive (and eliminate the negative") are not necessarily bad songs to keep spinning around in your mind – unless they create a fantasy world for you and lead you to deny the realities of existence with which all of us must deal. Being positive rather than negative has nothing to do with ignoring the challenges that are built into our existence as human beings living in an imperfect world. Atul Gawande in *Being Mortal* brings a wake-up call early in his book with the statement: "I asked Silverstone whether gerontologists have discerned any particular, reproducible pathway to aging. 'No,' he said, 'We just fall apart.'"[14]

No one wants to hear that, but I have an innumerable host who would quickly give a one-word response to that declaration: "Amen!" And, yet, popular speakers and ministers continue to give the recipes denying the normal ravishes that usually accompany old age, not always to the same degree and heavily based on how the person has lived and is living during the senior years. Much does depend on how we handle aging and there is truly some good news not based on wishing or repeating formulas as suggested in Joel Osteen's *I Declare: 32 Promises to Speak Over Your Life*. Brent Strawn gives this Day 1 declaration from the book:

> I DECLARE God's incredible blessings over my life. I will see an explosion of God's goodness, a sudden widespread increase. I'll experience the surpassing greatness of God's favor. It will elevate me to a level high than I dreamed of. Explosive blessings are coming my way. This is my declaration.[15]

Following this quote, Strawn makes this comment: "The verbal articulation makes reality happen – there is nothing to do but to

---

14 Gawande, Atul. *Being Mortal* (New York: Metropolitan Books, 2014), 35.

15   Strawn, Brent A. *The Old Testament is Dying* (Grand Rapids: Baker Academic, 2017), 134, 137.

Declare health. Declare favor. Declare abundance," because "you give life to your faith by what you say."[16] I certainly believe that words matter but the biblical teaching is that we give life to our faith by what we do. Have you ever wondered why the Sermon on the Mount ends with a crash and not an "Amen!"? Jesus teaches that everyone who hears his words and puts them into practice is like a wise person who builds a house on solid rock, but the foolish person is the one who hears his words and does not put them into practice. When the storms and floods of life come, the wise person's house stands and the foolish person's house comes down with a great crash. (Matthew 7:24-27).

Mary O'Brien in *Successful Aging* tells the readers: "The secrets that follow can benefit teenagers and retirees alike. Aging well is not a matter of luck. Aging well is a choice."[16] Her secrets all have to do with choices involving the actions we take.

But What About the Miracle Claims I See Widely Advertised?

In the May 2017 Costco magazine there was an "article" (with the note "PAID ADVERTISEMENT" at the top of the page), entitled: *Sero Vital…the Fastest Selling "Anti-Aging" Breakthrough in America!* This article was underneath a red-ended black box with white lettering: "Anti-Aging Update." The ad claims that their oral compound will actually stimulate the body's own production of what is called the "Youth Hormone." It claims to be clinically validated but a note at the bottom of the page notes: "These statements have not been evaluated by the Food and Drug Administration." A statement in large print at the top of the adjoining page reads: "Let's face it…anything that has a chance of reducing wrinkles, tightening saggy skin, decreasing body fat, increasing lean muscle mass, strengthening bones, and boosting mood, while giving you plenty of energy is…at the very least…irresistible."[17]

16 O'Brien, Mary. *SUCCESSFUL AGING* (Concord, CA: Biomed General, 2005),
17 "The Costco Connection," May, 2017, 102-103.

I do not doubt that some benefits have been experienced by some who have taken this product. My complaint is that it leads too many to believe that an anti-aging remedy is just a pill away and that successful aging can be accomplished without the conscious effort and hard work that all medical research says is necessary. I don't believe I have ever bought a book that promises "The quick and easy way to…." I did purchase the book that began with the sentence: "Life is difficult." The book, of course, is Scott Peck's bestseller *The Road Less Traveled.* Here is his reason for beginning the book in such an unusual way:

> I am often asked why I began my first book with the sentence: "Life is difficult." My answer is always, Because I wanted to combat the Lie. The Lie is that we are here on earth to be comfortable, happy, and fulfilled. Is that not our very purpose for being?
>
> The truth is that our finest moments are most likely to occur when we are feeling deeply uncomfortable, unhappy, and unfilled. For it is only in such moments, propelled by our discomfort, that we are likely to step out of our ruts and start searching for different ways or truer answers – or even for God.[18]

ARE DIRE STRAITS NECESSARY FOR AN AUTHENTIC REALITY CHECK?

In his book *The Courage for Truth,* Thomas Merton asks a question that caused me to do a great deal of rethinking: "Do we have to be in the concentration camp before the truth comes home to us?" Stories abound from those who made amazing discoveries about what really matters in life and where priorities ought to be while incarcerated in the hellish camps of Nazi Germany. (We will later cite one of the most famous examples). Those who claim to have had near death experiences confess to making the same kind of discoveries.

---

18 Peck, M. Scott. *An Anthology of Wisdom*, 23.

Do we have to wait until some great tragedy in life or for some chronic disease to remind of what is of real value in the earthly life we now enjoy? We shouldn't – but we often do. Perhaps the biggest reality check of all is the concluding one of this introduction:

> Your quality of life in old age will be an accumulation of
> the habits, beliefs, experiences and attitudes you've collected
> as you go through life.
>
> As you know, you won't suddenly arrive at old age. It will
> be merely an extension of who you are now, what happens to
> you along the way, and whatever changes you make to improve
> your life.[19]

My fear is that the elderly will be the only ones to read this book, that others will not see aging as an issue for them. They are totally unaware of the anonymous quote I found years ago: "We may not *be* aged, but we are, at our best, heading in that direction."

QUESTIONS FOR REFLECTION, DISCOVERY, AND CONVERSATION

1. Have you ever tried an "anti-aging" product? What were the results?
2. What was your reaction to the choice of "post-truth" as the 2016 word of the year?
3. What was the most important reality check in this chapter for you?

---

19   Creagan, Edward T. ed., *Mayo Clinic on Healthy Aging,* 8, 14.

LEARNING TO LIVE WITH INCREASING LOSSES AND LIMITATIONS

SETTING THE STAGE

Modes of repair are shut down progressively as we age.[20]

(It began with persistent lower back pain). Probably require some therapy, I thought, never considering it could be anything more than an over exercised back. The conceit of a long, lucky life is that bad things happen to others.[21]

Old age is a continuous series of losses.[22]

20 Mitteldorf, Josh & Dorion Sagan. *Cracking the Code* (New York: Flatiron books, 2016), 35.
21 Brokaw, Tom. *A Lucky Life Interrupted* (New York: Random House, 2015), 4.
22 Gawande, Atul. *Being Mortal*, 55.

WE ARE REALLY CONTINUING OUR REALITY CHECK WITH THE TWO BIG L's

It may seem as though this book will be a confession like the one I received from a eighty-eight year old woman I visited in the hospital. She was known as a pleasant and positive person. When I entered the room I gave my usual opening statement: "Well, tell me how things are going." To my surprise, she quickly came back, "Don't let anybody fool you. Old age is Hell!" Then there was a pause and she continued, "Well, now that that's over, we can have a good visit!" And we did.

That woman was not expressing her philosophy but was simply giving voice to the frustrations that can come when aging deals its two biggest cards: loss and limitation. Only two nights ago in a conversation with a retired surgeon who is almost ninety, he confessed that he was feeling down because in one week he had lost two of his medical friends, two of his best friends. This coincides with what I have heard far too often from older members of a congregation: "It seems like all I do is go to funeral homes."

They are in no way implying that friendships are not worth making or that life is not worth living. They are acknowledging one of the two great realities that none of us want to acknowledge. The losses do pile up as the years unfold and life challenges us with limits that restrict and make our worlds smaller than we wish.

But do not despair! In this first chapter we complete setting the stage for all the helpful, positive, and beneficial things we *can* do to make our later years creative, productive, fulfilling, purposeful, and even hopeful. My personal faith and my decades of preaching, carry the message that our God is not in the demolition and elimination business. Our God is the God of preservation, reclamation, reconstruction, and resurrection. Much more on these subjects will come later in the book.

The rest of this book is not only good news, it is *great* news, because there is so much we *can* do to make our "golden" years have some of that glitter that *is* intended. I do believe that in almost every situation it is possible to have at least some of the "good old age" that is noted in the life of Abraham (Genesis 25:8). So, just a little more reality until we come to even greater and brighter realities.

IT IS NOT JUST IN THE LATER YEARS BUT IN ALL OF OUR YEARS

All of life has its limitations and losses. How do we handle the losses that begin piling up as we age? The key is to learn how to successfully negotiate the losses that arrive early in life and come in all shapes and sizes. A vivid example of how to handle early losses comes from a most unexpected source – the 1982 movie *Poltergeist* which the Chicago Film Critic Association named the twentieth scariest film ever made.

The scene I want to recall is not "scary." It is instructive and redemptive. Before the horror really begins, there is an episode in which the mother, Diane, discovers her daughter's pet canary dead at the bottom of its cage. She prepares to dispose of Tweety as she holds it above the commode in the bathroom, when suddenly she sees young Carol Ann standing wide-eyed at the door. In the next scene we witness mother and daughter placing the canary in a cigar box, placing a "blanket" over him, putting in a photograph of the family, and laying a flower on top. Following the burial of the box in the yard, Carol Ann seems satisfied that the canary has been given an appropriate sendoff.

Rather than simply announcing, "Don't worry, we'll get another canary," Diane participates in a ceremony acknowledging the loss, preparing for a more dignified departure than a mere "flush," and recognizing the significance of this small bird in the life of her daughter. Each loss is unique, each situation is different, and the persons involved deal with the situation in a complex way involving many factors and past circumstances. The grief experience for youngsters must be "tailor-made" as it must be for all of us wherever we are in life.

When some people discover that more than one-half of the Psalms come under the heading "Psalms of Lament," they wonder how this could happen in the hymn book and prayer book of a "people of faith." The value of lament is generally ignored (and often suppressed) in a culture like ours. We simply want to "get on with it" and live as though the loss never occurred. But especially with the loss of people we love, life will *never* be the same again and constructing our lives with a vacant chair forever at the table is no easy matter. Grieving our loss, feeling the pain, and taking time to experience all the emotions that come to us, are essential in the grieving process. The psalms provide excellent models for giving voice to the hurt and lament that need to be felt and expressed. Two of the best lines I have read on this subject come from a book titled *Bearing the Unbearable:* "Lament is faith's alternate to despair. Lament risks everything on God."[23]

"You Can Do Anything You Want to Do and Be Anything You Want to Be"

When I hear the above phrase, I want to shout, "Not true!" All through life there are limitations we have based on many factors, including: genes, motivation, desire, commitment, persistence, talents (gifts), inherent disabilities, and opportunity. The two lists, "Can Do" and "Can't Do" are not clear cut. I always add a third one: "The Possibility List." Some things are attainable with enough effort and hard work. Often that is due to the passion we feel about something: "It is in me and I simply have to do it!" I would say, "Go for it!"

The remainder of this book is about deciding to take a proactive approach to aging and determining at no point along the way to assume the role of victim. Almost always there is something we can do – even in situations that seem beyond any alternative except to succumb to the circumstances. There are losses and there are limitations – period. How we handle them is always optional.

23 Hunsinger, Deborah Van Duesen. *Bearing the Unbearable* (Grand Rapids: William B. Eerdmans, 2015), 83.

QUESTIONS FOR REFLECTION, DISCOVERY, AND CONVERSATION

1. How did you handle the early losses in your life?
2. What are the present limitations in your life that are giving you the most difficulties?
3. Have you felt the increase of losses as you have aged? How have you dealt with these?

ONE THING WE ALWAYS DO IS WHAT WE SHOULD ALWAYS DO

Events do not have meanings. Events are events, and meanings are thoughts. Nothing has any meaning save the meaning you give it. And the meaning you give to things does not derive from any event, circumstance, condition, or situation exterior to yourself. The Giving of Meaning is entirely an internal process. Entirely.[24]

Perception appears to be automatic, but, in fact, it is a learned phenomenon.[25]

Becca R. Levy, a psychiatrist at Yale, has found striking correlations between people's attitudes toward old age and how they fare in their later years, with effects starting as early as middle age.[26]

---

24 Walsch, Neale Donald. *When Everything Changes, Change Everything* (Ashland, OR: EmNin Books, 2009), 79.
25 Chopra, Deepak. *Ageless Body, Timeless Mind*, 6.
26 Leland, John. *Happiness is a Choice You Make* (New York: Sarah Crichton Books, 2018), 203.

It's Always the Place to Begin

In outlining what is termed "The Eight Pillars of Joy," The Dalai Lama and Desmond Tutu list *Perspective* as number one.

> (Perspective means) our ability to reframe our situation more positively. Our capacity to experience gratitude and our choice to be kind and generous. A healthy perspective really is the foundation of joy and happiness, because the way we see the world is the way we experience the world ... The way you look at the world, the meaning you give to what you witness, changes the way you feel.[27]

The most famous, and the most unbelievable, testimony to this truth comes from Victor Frankl's classic work, *Man's Search for Meaning*, about life in a Nazi death camp:

> In the concentration camp every circumstances conspires to make the prisoner lose his hold. All the familiar goals in life are snatched away. What alone remains is "the last of human freedoms" – the ability to "choose one's attitude in a given set of circumstances."[28]

The challenge for me is the reminder: if you can do it here, you can do it anywhere, under any circumstances. When I refuse to believe and practice this I have given up the one human freedom that nobody can take away from me. (Or to rephrase it, I have given up the one human responsibility that always belongs to me. In Chapter 14 we will explore the one phrase that still lies at the heart of our human condition: personal responsibility.)

The Story of Two Amazing Women

Two of the greatest realists I ever knew when it came to aging and two of the liveliest were two members of my congregation

---

27   The Dali Lama, Desmond Tutu, and Douglas Abrams, *The Book of Joy* (New York: Avery, 2016), 194, 196.

28   Frankl, Victor E. *Man's Search for Meaning* (Boston: Beacon Press, 1959), xi.

in Waynesboro, Virginia: Anna Young and Lucille Davis. They were both in their eighties and no word can describe them except: delightful. No one ever gave a party in this relatively small town without inviting both of them. On one occasion, we were all standing in line at a reception and I overheard the following exchange between them:

> Anna to Lucille: How are you?
> Lucille: Deteriorating gradually. How are you?
> Anna: Fine…although a family member calls me every morning to see if I'm dead.
> Lucille: Have you ever been?
> Anna: I thought I was once…but I wasn't!

No, neither of them had ever been dead! They were full of life and fun and joy! But I don't want you to think for a moment that life had been easy for either of them. Anna's husband had died at a fairly young age and for many years she had cared for a Down's Syndrome son. Likewise, Lucille's doctor husband had been dead for many years and she had a son who suffered from many emotional problems and couldn't hang on to a job anywhere. And these were just the troubles at the tip of the iceberg.

But that day at a reception you would have thought they didn't have a care in the world as they celebrated one of life's great occasions with friends. They never denied any part of the reality of their lives…including the growing old part. They accepted change and loss as a part of life. It wasn't quick or easy, but they did it.

THE PROBLEM OF "HALO EFFECTS"

By halo effect I mean that to know of someone's past biases our judgment of their present. An ordinary wine tastes very different if poured from a bottle with a Chateau Lafitte label than from a screw-top jug labeled Thunderbird.[29]

---

29 Valliant, George E. *Aging Well,* 34.

A recent news story brought shock (and a total refund) to those involved in an experiment conducted by a bargain discount shoe company. They opened a store in an upscale shopping area and brought in much of the same stock that was carried in the discount store. The only difference was, this time the merchandise was given outrageous mark-ups, some into the several hundred dollar category. Many of the buyers were asked to evaluate their purchase and commented on the exceptional quality and design of the shoe they had just purchased. The information that it could be purchased at a fraction of the cost at the bargain store left them speechless.

The halo effect written in the book *Ageing Well* by a physician only confirms that packaging, expectation, and ever-present biases can be applied to much more than a bottle of wine. I repeat a quote from the beginning of this chapter: "Perception appears to be automatic, but in fact it is a learned phenomenon."[30] "I know a quality shoe when I see one," is not an accurate statement. Rather, "My past experiences and the perceptions and measurements I used for determining quality is the standard I continue to use."

IF ONLY THINGS WERE DIFFERENT!

"The real voyage of discovery consists not in seeking new landscape, but in having new eyes" (Marcel Proust). The writer who gives this citation then maintains that when you change the vantage point, you change the frame. Watching a football game from above the stadium, not at the fifty-yard line literally gives you a new set of eyes.[31] Being able to see things differently calls for changing our frame of reference, literally getting a new perspective, and keeping our eyes new because we are always trying to view things from different angles and different points of view. (Sounds like a lot of work, doesn't it? It is!)

One of my must-read recommendations is Huston Smith's *Tales of Wonder*. The epilogue, "Reflections on Turning Ninety," is

---

30   Chopra, Deepak. Ageless Body, Timeless Mind, 6.
31   Steinke, Peter L. *Teaching Fish to Walk* (Austin: New Vision Press, 2016), 21-23.

worth the price of the book and is, as far as I am concerned, one of the greatest tales of wonder I have ever read. After an extremely active life and a period of increasing physical needs, Smith found himself in an assisted--living facility. He writes:

> The first night after the move was a dark night of the soul. Religion relies on that successful plot device, the happy ending. I still believed in one, but after my first night in the assisted-living residence, I thought, "The happy ending will now have to wait until I am dead."
>
> And then after three days there, it became acceptable, perfectly fine. The move seemed no more than turning the page of a book. On the previous page I had been on Colusa Avenue and on this page I am here....
>
> People go to nursing homes, I've heard it said, to die. I came to this assisted-living residence, it seems, to cheer people up. I still begin each day with exercise for the body, reading religious classics for my mind, and prayer for the spirit....I have added a fourth practice. Mentally I take a census of the other residents here, and as each appears in my imagination, I ask how I might improve his or her day.[32]

The book gives many more details of this story of wonder. It underscores one of the continuing emphases of this book: With new eyes and new perspectives, there is really no limit to the tales of wonder we can produce in our own lives.

QUESTIONS FOR REFLECTION, DISCOVERY, AND CONVERSATION

1. What was your initial reaction to Huston Smith's narrative of his nursing home experience?
2. Do you agree that perspective and our ability to choose are options always open to us?
3. Do you recall times when the "halo effect" shaped an evaluation or a decision?

---

32 Smith, Houston *Tales of Wonder* (New York: HarperOne, 2009), 177-180.

CHAPTER 3

WHAT IS YOUR DEFAULT SETTING?

...we have absorbed a climate of opinion that modifies the weather of our thinking.[33]

Self-centeredness is most of our default perspective.[34]

Sometimes, the hardest part in learning something new is unlearning the old way of doing it.[35]

Your de facto world view determines what you pay attention to and what you don't notice at all. It's largely unconscious and it drives you to do this and not that.[36]

---

33 Shideler, Mary McDermott. *In Search of the Spirit* (New York: Ballantine Books, 1985), 162.
34 The Dalai Lama, Desmond Tutu, and Douglas Abrams, *The Book of Joy,* 198.
35 McGraw, Phillip C. *Life Strategies,* 41.
36 Rohr, Richard. with Jon Bookser Feister, *Hope Against Darkness* (Cincinnati: St. Anthony Messenger Press, 2001), 125.

Our Perceptual Filters

This is our bridge from the last chapter because it speaks to how often we are unaware of the influences that impinge (or even dictate) on what we see, what we hear, and the interpretations we make of events. In her book *Visual Intelligence: Sharper Your Perception, Change Your Life,* Amy Herman gives a list of self-check items to help us determine how accurate our perceptions really are. Her question is : Am I Being Influenced by…[37]

- — my own experiences or the experiences of those close to me?
- — my geographic history, affinity, or present location?
- — my values, morals, culture, or religious beliefs?
- — my upbringing or education?
- — my professional desires, ambitions, or failures?
- — my personal desires, ambitions, or failures?
- — my inherent likes or dislikes?
- — my financial experience or outlook?
- — my political beliefs?
- — my physical state (illness, height, weight, et cetera)?
- — my current mood?
- — groups I identify with and organizations I belong to?
- — media that I've consumed: books, television, websites?
- — information or impressions passed on to me by a friend or colleague?

"Do you want to change the default setting?" is the computer's reminder that there is one and that it is possible to change it with the click of a button. It's not quite so easy in the larger realms of life. My thesis is that there is almost always a default setting – we need to be aware of what it is and what components go into it.

---

37 Herman, Amy E. *Visual Intelligence* (Boston: An Eamon Dolan Book, 2016), 48-49.

Rules for Working with (and Around) Our Biases

When Jesus announced, "Blessed are those who have ears to hear; blessed are those who have eyes to see," many in the crowd must have wondered, "Isn't that what we're doing right now?" For those who believed that "nothing good could come out of Nazareth (John 1:46)," their hearing was impaired and their vision distorted when it came to assessing Jesus and his message. They didn't have eyes to see or ears to hear and didn't know it.

Many years ago, I was the guest minister in a church in England. In the course of my sermon I used a quotation from Leslie Weatherhead. Only later did I discover that single sentence shut down the listening for a large portion of the congregation and sent word through the small town that the guest minister was a heretic. The quote was quite orthodox. Many are unaware that Weatherhead's *The Will of God* is one of the best books ever written on the subject and is widely recommended across the spectrum of Christian thinking. There is much Weatherhead wrote that challenges traditional beliefs but that does not mean he never had anything of value to say to the larger community, unless you believe that "nothing good can come from Weatherhead."

To say there was a bias against this English clergyman is an understatement. I was wiped away (figuratively and literally!) by the firestorm the very mention of his name set loose. This seems a good place to insert some helpful information on the subject. In *Visual Intelligence* the author gives three rules for working with and around our biases:

> Rule 1: Become Aware of Our Biases and Boot the Bad Ones. Our biases exist because we're hard-wired to make unconscious decisions about others based on what we instantly perceive as safe, sane, or comfortable.

> Rule 2: Don't Mistake Biases for Facts; Instead Use Them to Find Facts. Our biases are not veri-

*fied facts. They are feelings and experiences that
make us want to believe something, but they aren't
enough to create a conclusion. Instead, use them as
a starting point to look further.*

*Rule 3: Run Our Conclusions Past Others. We need
others to help us discern which of our conclusions
are faulty and which are not.*[38]

PAYING TOO MUCH ATTENTION TO THE WRONG INFORMATION

I know people who get all their "information" from social media or talk-shows. The danger of such an approach is highlighted in
Bill Nye's *Everything All At Once*: "YouTube abounds with videos
showing evidence of NASA's UFO cover-ups or proving conclusive-
ly that the Earth is flat. I worry that they (we) are still stuck in the
mindset of paying too much attention to the wrong information."[39]

Nye cites Carl Sagan who refers to critical thinking as a "baloney detections kit." Nye adds: "For me, there are three key ideas
in thinking critically about a claim that you come across. First, Is
it specific? Second: Is it based on the simplest interpretation of
the phenomenon? And third: Has it been independently verified?[40]
We are all familiar with the quote: "The unexamined life is not
with living." I add my twist to that: "The unexamined thought is
not worth having."

"I heard the other day," or "Someone told me" are illustrations
of unprocessed ideas. In a later chapter we are going to spend some
time discussing "reflection" as something more than just religious
contemplation. Reflection gives us time to analyze, process, or (as
my Dad used to say) mull things over. Seniors are quite capable of
doing critical thinking if we believe that the accumulated years may
mean the lack of ability to recall specific information but almost
always brings the richer treasure of wisdom. With that wisdom we

---

38   Ibid., 254f.
39   Nye, Bill. *Everything All At Once* (New York: Rodale, 2017), 189, 200.
40   Ibid., 190.

are able to do critical thinking that should mark all of life but is especially necessary in dealing with the challenges of our later years.

WHAT ABOUT A DIFFERENT KIND OF DEFAULT SETTING?

"While aging is inevitable, how you will age is often largely up to you. Aging invites you to have discernment."[41] This observation from Alan Wolfert (one of my favorite workshop presenters) has given me my idea for the best default setting for seniors: "Discernment." You immediately know this is not something that automatically positions you in the correct seeing and feeling mode but requires time (reflection) and active decision-making. We don't have to rush into responses. The best response to a classic question comes from an unremembered source: "How are you?" Response: "How soon do you have to know?" That can be a legitimate response because you're not quite certain how you ought to respond. (I never give the oft heard answer: "I'm still above ground," which I do not count as much of a response.)

In a seminar for ministers, the speaker set the stage by using this brief story: "I think I know how many of us often begin our day. We make certain we have a time for some Scripture reading, meditation, and prayer, then after other necessary preparations rush out the door to begin a full-schedule. Suddenly we notice that we have a flat tire. How often have we said, 'Oh, no! This is going to ruin my whole day!' With that being said, we are assured that it will."

If discernment is my default setting, there are other possibilities than seeing a flat tire as a major calamity. Pausing, we might reflect: "Well, I certainly hadn't counted on this! I'll have to give my first appointment a call to let him know I'll be a little late." We then either change the tire or call AAA. (I am a fifty year member and it has been a lifesaver for me on more than one occasion.) It has put a wrinkle in our day but whoever has a wrinkle free day?

---

41   Wolfelt, Alan D. & Kirby J. Duvall, *Healing Your Grief About Aging*. 4.

Keeping Resilience in Our Lives

Many have echoed the idea, "It doesn't matter how many times you fall, it's how many times you get up that counts," but none better than Eric Greitens in his book, *Resilience:*

> For most of history, our feet were hardened by walking on the rough ground. In our world, most people wear shoes. Shoes are good. They protect our feet. But we realize that it is possible to gain something very good and still lose something very real. What most of us have lost is the ability to walk barefoot over difficult ground.
>
> Today, sheltered from hardships of hunger, disease, heat and cold that stalked human life for centuries, some people have lost their capacity to deal with real difficulty. Growing up in a protected palace of comfort, they have lost their ability to walk through pain.[42]

We all need this ability and we are impoverished by those who seek to protect us from pain (or such walking). I question the wisdom of parents who refuse to allow their children to attend funerals. If they don't walk through the pain of loss, how will they handle the severe losses of later life that come without parental protection? The Scriptures overflow with descriptions of God bringing his people *through* pain, of God lifting them up after they have fallen, of God rescuing them from captivity and bondage of all kinds, of God delivering from weights and woes of all descriptions. You're going to be hard pressed to find the major teaching of the Bible to be: Don't worry. If you belong to God, he won't let anything bad happen to you.

Please don't take this section of material to be a prophecy of doom and gloom for aging. Absolutely not! (Sidebar: There is usually some of that doom and gloom sprinkled throughout life!) The intent is to underscore the basic truth of this entire book: The most important thing is not *what* happens to me but *how I handle* what happens to me. I am not my circumstances; what I am is

---

42   Grietens, Eric. *Resilience* (Boston: Mariner Books, 2015), 138.

determined by how I respond to my circumstances. I may not be able to determine the outcome, but it is always in my power to determine my attitude and my behavior along the way.

QUESTIONS FOR REFLECTION, DISCOVERY, AND CONVERSATION

1. How many in the list of perception filters did you recognize as yours?
2. What about Bill Nye's equating critical thinking with a "baloney detection kit?"
3. How do you keep resilience in your life?

4

Do You Aim for Control
or Guidance?

*Nothing suffocates the life force more thoroughly
than trying to control what is happening.*[43]

*Before I continue with my own personal story, let
me give you some idea of where I'm heading. It's all
about control. Control is illusory. No matter what
university you go to, no matter what degree you
hold, if your goal is to become master of your own
destiny you have more to learn. Parkinson's is a per-
fect metaphor for lack of control. Michael J. Fox.*[44]

Recognition of Another Reality

When I began pastoral ministry it was not uncommon for
churches to prepare a five-year plan. When I began interim ministry I would routinely ask for copies of any plans the church had
made. On more than one occasion I was informed, "We did an

---

43 Arrien, Angeles. *The Second Half of Life* (Boulder: Sounds True, 2005),
169.
44 Fox, Michael J. *A Funny Thing Happened On the Way to the Future* (New
York: Hyperion, 2010), 84.

extensive study several years ago and came up with a five-year plan. I think it's in the closet in the pastor's study." No comment is necessary except to add that most planning today may involve "a strategy for the coming year" with a three-month fairly detailed agenda for implementing that strategy. There's not an area you can name that is not experiencing rapid-fire changes coming from multiple directions. The aging are having the same experience.

Michael J. Fox has written the by-line that many of us have unofficially adopted: *A Funny Thing Happened on the Way to the Future.* All too often it is far from funny and that is the first thing you confront in Fox's challenging and courageous book about dealing with Parkinson's. Many of us have witnessed the determination and bravery that marked his limited return to acting and his leadership in raising money for Parkinson's research. It came as a total surprise early in his life. Those surprises just keep coming for those of us who are seniors.

If you are a lover of good poetry you might want to skip this next section which I originally dedicated to a good friend of mine with the notation: "Dedicated to one who knows bad poetry when he sees it." The impetus for writing such a piece came from my friend's report of driving along a rural road when suddenly a buzzard flew into his outside left mirror, careened across the hood of the car, and landed in a roadside ditch. His insurance agent believed his report but noted it was the first of its kind. I sent him this poem with my apologies:

> The sun was shining on a cloudless day.
> The road ahead was open all the way.
> All seemed bright and clear and good;
> In every way, the way it should.
>
> And suddenly, out of nowhere came
> a large black bird with reckless aim.
> He hit my car with quite a thud,
> and landed kerplunk in the roadside mud.

So now as you travel along your way,
be prepared for the unexpected in your day.
For you never know when you'll be next
and get hit by some unexpected hex.

And so the moral of this little tale
is to enable you to prevail
when out of the blue on a sun-filled day
some buzzard like thing comes winging your way.

In simple words: about the time we think we have some real control over our lives, the out of the blue, unexpected gives us a wakeup call.

DOES THAT MEAN WE DON'T MAKE PLANS?

Absolutely not! Plans, dreams, hopes, visions, etc. are a necessary part of any organization and of every phase of our lives. The warning is to avoid becoming like Mr. Banks in the original *Mary Poppins* who proudly sings that his life, like the bank, is run precisely on schedule. The children and their new nanny soon take care of that and at the end of the film we find him happily flying a kite with his children. The lesson of the film is not that all of life is to be lived with a lighthearted disregard for responsibility and commitments. It's the call to put a little serendipity in your schedule (or rather, allow it to happen). It's the call to be open to life, continuing to live by a larger plan.

Kay Carlish, a retired elementary school teacher who also worked in real estate, writes: "Reflecting back over my seventy-eight years, I realized that I have lived with serendipity. Stumbling blocks had become stepping stones to greater wisdom. Instead of saying, 'Woe is me,' wake up every morning saying, 'What do you have planned for us today, Lord?' and smile!"[45]

Kay continued teaching and working in real estate but she had flexibility built into her days. Michael J. Fox continued his acting career but it had some large stumbling stones that called for extraordinary flexibility. No one else in my family had ever attended college and my dad was determined that I should go. With very limited resources and four children, his resources were stretched beyond the limit. In ways (and jobs) I never imagined, I did manage to complete my college education and one year of seminary. A money crunch postponed continuing and through a number challenging years with unexpected birds of difficulty, I finally completely my education. It certainly was not precisely on schedule but the plan and the vision did not alter.

Richard Eyre has written an entire book on *Spiritual Serendipity.* The subtitle is: *Cultivating and Celebrating the Art of the Unexpected.* The word serendipity was coined by Horace Walpole who was inspired by the Persian Fable "The Three Princes of Serendip." (It is a tale well worth the read.) Eyre compares the original definition, "The quality or faculty, through awareness or good fortune, of being able to find something good while seeking something else," with Spiritual serendipity: "The same quality but with the added input and direction of spiritual receptivity and divine guidance."[46]

You will notice in both the secular and the religious framework something good is discovered while seeking something else. While pursuing your plan, goal, dream, etc. Serendipity is often referred to as "a happy accident" which comes to those who are actively pursuing something they already feel strongly compelled to do. "The goal is to shift from attitudes of control, manipulation, and self-determination to attitudes of awareness and guidance."[47]

---

45 Scott, Williard. *The Older the Fiddle, the Better the Tune* (New York: Hyperion, 2003), 54.

46 Eyre, Richard. *Spiritual Serendipity* (New York: Simon & Schuster, 1997), 5.

47 Ibid., 25.

PERHAPS THE QUAKERS HAVE IT RIGHT

Without realizing it, most of my life I have followed the Quaker Rule of Thumb: "Proceed as the way opens."[48] This naturally involves the attitudes of awareness and guidance mentioned by Richard Eyre. Especially as we age, I believe this is more important than ever. Paying attention to life is a large part of Chapter 16 (Learn to Live in the Now), but is an integral part of any concept of God's guidance in our lives. My experience is similar to this description: "Most believers…agree that God's answers usually come not in detailed instruction but in directional promptings or in feelings of light or calmness or clarity that confirm our own directions or inclinations when they are right."[49]

This means that I must be paying attention to what is happening around me – and within me. In reading about the life of Fred Rogers in *The Good Neighbor,* I found this highly instructive piece:

> The notion of "guided drift," that we're guided by our principles, but also free to embrace the flow of life, was one Fred Rogers made his own and shared with friends for the rest of his life. It strongly influenced his willingness to experiment and take chances in his career.[50]

This concept has nothing to do with aimless floating as you read about the life a man who was determined to make a difference in the media education of young children. The story is full of risks, problems, criticism from his peers, determination, and many rough times along the way, but his legacy is a testimony to the effectiveness of his kind of drift. Rogers was alert and sensitive and as the way opened, he moved forward. He never kicked down any doors but he certainly knocked and prayed that they would be opened. He then proceeded through the ones that did open.

---

48   Shideler, Mary McDermott. *In Search of the Spirit*, 162.
49   Eyre, Richard. Spiritual Serendipity, 137.
50   King, Maxwell. *The Good Neighbor* (New York: Abrams Press, 2018), 118.

THE ONE PLACE CONTROL NEVER WORKS

One of my basic rules for good relationships and maintaining personal peace and serenity is my declaration: "I'm into input; I'm not into outcome." I have read in multiple publications, in one form or another, the phrase: "All spirituality is about mastering the art of letting go." Meaning: we do what we can to the best of our ability under the present circumstances and, then, we let it go. We place it in God's hands. Regardless of how things turn out, this attitude means we will be much better equipped to deal with whatever comes down the pike. Majoring on outcomes and not input keeps us twisted in the knotty world of "if only," "what if," "why didn't I," and "this is not what should have happened."

Too many of the letters I see in the advice column that appears in our local newspaper describe the irritable or destructive behavior of a relative or friend. The question the reader asks can be boiled down to, "What can I do to cause this person to change that behavior?" Usually the person sending the letter is at wits' end – the place you usually wind up when you major on outcomes.

In his *The Little Book of Letting Go,* Hugh Prather has these lines under the heading "Letting Go of Outcomes":

> Although we can't control even the tiniest ego or smallest event, we can control our decision to control. It always breaks our connection with another person to say anything that causes that individual to become defensive or self-conscious.[51]

When we give up our decision to control, to craft our words and actions in order to bring about a desired outcome for the other person, we are free to say and do those things a caring, loving, and considerate person would offer to someone who doesn't have it all together (and who does?). The freedom that comes when you give up being the "fixer" is a freedom that too many will never experience because they are convinced it is their job to do just that. No. It is my job to relate to you as another human being who

---

51   Prather, Hugh. *The Little Book of Letting Go* (New York: MJF Books, 2000), 112, 160.

diagnose

demonstrates care and concern without attempting to ~~diagnosis~~ and prescribe remedies for your "condition" as I understand it.

The older I get the more I realize how little I have ever had control over and just how much I have needed guidance from a resource outside of myself. Teachers, counselors, advisors, friends, co-workers, and minister friends have all provided light and encouragement for specific transitions in my journey. Always, however, prayer, meditation, Scripture and devotional reading, and reliance on that "still small voice" of the Spirit within have been instruments for guidance. As for knowing what was best to do, I have found that "proceeding as the way opens" continues to be the most logical and spiritual approach.

QUESTIONS FOR REFLECTION, DISCOVERY, AND CONVERSATION

1. What events in your life helped to shatter the illusion of control? Or do you still live with that same illusion?
2. What are some of the buzzard like things that have come winging their way into your life?
3. How did you respond to the Quaker Rule of Thumb: "Proceed as the way opens"?

Chapter 5

TAKE TWO LAUGHS AND CALL ME IN THE MORNING

SETTING THE STAGE

> *Loretta LaRoche writes in her 1998 book Relax: You May Only Have a Few Minutes Left, "No one ever said on his deathbed, 'I wish I hadn't laughed so much.'"*[52]

> *The average preschool child laughs over 350 times a day. The average adult laughs about ten. Why? Because children come into the world with clean refrigerators!*[53]

> *New Yorker cartoon: Two very elderly men sitting on a bench. One turns to the other and says, "My inner child just turned sixty-five."*[54]

> *"A cheerful heart is good medicine, but a crushed spirit dries up the bones." (Proverbs 17:22).*

---

52 Creagan, Edward T. ed., *Mayo Clinic on Healthy Aging*, 14.
53 Prather, Hugh. *The Little Book of Letting Go*, 26.
54 Scott, Williard. *The Older the Fiddle, the Better the Tune*, 68.

A Good Medicine for Every Day in the Year

Dr. Clifford Kuhn, a Louisville native, is known as "The Laugh Doctor." He describes himself this way:

> I am the laugh doctor, a psychiatrist who for decades now has researched humor's *physiological* and psychological powers. A professor and former Associate Chairman of the University of Louisville Medical School's Department of Psychiatry, I have studied the healing effects of laughter from an academic perspective, from my own medical case studies and from working (and playing) with such world famous humor practitioners as comedian Jerry Lewis, Dr. Patch Adams...Allen Klein, best-selling author and past president of the Association for Applied and Therapeutic humor, and Dr. Steven Wilson, the founder and guiding spirit of The World Laughter Tour.[55]

Based on his research, Dr. Kuhn has developed a highly successful HA HA HA Prescription which capitalizes on laughter's ability to heal. It is a three-phase formula for unleashing the healing power of your humor nature (not a typo!) in every situation. The three HA'S stand for: Humor Attitude, Humor Aptitude, and Humor Action. His book *It All Starts With a Smile* explains how to take this prescription.[56]

Most will remember Norman Cousins' discovery that ten minutes of deep laughter, as he watched old Marx Brothers movies, would give him two hours of pain-free sleep. I have read that some hospitals have what is known as "Laugh Wagons" that contain DVDs of funny movies. Leonard Sweet tells that in India laughter has been made into a form of medical therapy through "laughing clubs." It is nothing less than organized giggling once a week for what is called the "laughing cure." The first laughing club opened in 1994 and hundreds have been started since.[57]

---

55 Kuhn, Clifford. *It All Starts With a Smile* (Louisville: Butler Books, 2007), 1.
56 Ibid., 5.
57 Sweet, Leonard. *Soul Salsa* (Grand Rapids: Zondervan, 2000), 188-189.

WHAT WE ARE NOT SAYING

When we talk about humor and laughter a word of caution is always in order.

> A nervous young woman fidgeted in her chair. It was clear she did not want to be in a psychiatrist's consulting room.
>
> "I'll be honest with you Dr. Kuhn. The only reason I'm here is because I respect Dr. Adams, my oncologist....She calls you the Laugh Doctor. If you're planning to tell me I can laugh away my cancer, I'll just leave right now."
>
> "I don't see anything funny about breast cancer," I said quietly. "However, I have discovered this to be true. If you can hold onto your sense of humor while you are going through the surgery, the chemotherapy, the fear, uncertainty and pain of it all, you'll do better, live longer and have a better quality of life. If you'll let me, I'd like to help you keep your sense of humor."[58]

I am certainly not advocating laughing away the tragedies of life. I am not advocating refusing to face loss and the accompanying grief and pain that are a part of it. I am not advocating inappropriate humor to get troubled or grieving people into a happy mood! Nothing I can think of is more insensitive than not meeting others where they are in the struggles, disappointments, and tragedies of life. According to Ecclesiastes 3:4: *(There is) a time to weep and a time to laugh, a time to mourn and a time to dance....*Even in the midst of that weeping and mourning comes a challenging idea that calls for consideration and much reflection. From a chapter about the value of humor with the sick and the dying comes this idea:

> "Humor breaks the frame, attesting to something that transcends present limits. It is a glimmer of redemption. For a moment we burst out of life's boundaries."[59]

---

58 Kuhn, Clifford. *The Fun Factor* (Louisville: Minerva Books, 2002), 12.
59 Fischer, Kathleen. *Imaging Life After Death* (New York: Paulist Press, 2004), 100.

WHY ISN'T THERE MORE LAUGHTER IN THE BIBLE?

Almost everyone knows the shortest verse in the Bible: *"Jesus wept"* (John 11:35). A literal translation from the Greek tells us more: *Jesus burst into tears.* There is not a single reference in the Gospels where Jesus laughs. Much, however, can be inferred from some of the stories Jesus tells that could only have brought laughter to those who heard them. For instance, the picture of someone running around peering into the eyes of his neighbors looking for specks of sawdust while he has a log protruding out of his own eye is ridiculous! I don't see how Jesus could have told this with a straight face. The fact that Jesus and his disciples are invited to a big wedding at Cana and the shocking fact (to many!) that Jesus produces between 120 and 150 gallons of wine after the supply is exhausted speaks volumes. A wedding was a gala affair lasting several days in the lives of people who often had little to celebrate. The host must have made certain that only party enhancers, not party subtractors would make up the guest list. That first group included Jesus and his disciples.

Many are dismayed that the only references to God laughing are connected with his mocking those who foolishly flaunt their own power or seek to live as though they are accountable only to themselves. An example of this is Psalm 2:4. After describing nations that conspire and plot against the Lord's anointed, the psalmist writes: *"The One enthroned in heaven laughs...."*

The biblical frame of reference I keep in mind is that two of the great role models of faith in Hebrews 11 were great laughers – even at times when it might seem inappropriate to us. In the Genesis saga, when Abraham is told that he and Sarah are going to have a child, he has such a fit of laughter that he doubles over and falls on the ground. After all, he is 100 and Sarah is 90. So he laughs – right in front of God. Later, when Sarah hears the ludicrous promise, she laughs too. And what does God do? He tells them to name the child who will be born Isaac. And what does the name Isaac mean? Laughter! Abraham laughs and Sarah laughs and God laughs with them!

One of my favorite pieces is from the fourteenth-century Dominican mystic, Meister Eckhart:

> *Do you want to know*
> *what goes on in the core of the Trinity?*
> *I will tell you.*
> *In the core of the Trinity*
> *the Father laughs*
> *and gives birth to the Son.*
> *The Son laughs back at the Father*
> *and gives birth to the Spirit.*
> *The whole Trinity laughs*
> *and gives birth to us.*[60]

I am fully convinced that the music of heaven is laughter.

BASICALLY, HUMOR LIGHTENS AND ENLIVENS EVERYTHING

During the Second World War many of the children were taken to outlying areas where they could be safe from the nightly London blitz. One of those taken to the home of C.S. Lewis was Patricia Heidelberger who recorded her initial experience:

> My first impression of C. S. Lewis was that of a shabbily clad, rather portly gentleman, whom I took to be the gardener, and told him so. He roared – boomed – with laughter. And then with a twinkle in his eye, he said, "Welcome, girls."[61]

In the context of the star status of Lewis at this time, it speaks volumes that, rather than getting on the defensive, he laughed at himself. Even though he took his writing very seriously, he never took himself too seriously. The children who temporarily lived at the Kilns were indeed a blessed group. During the most dangerous

---

60 Rohr, Richard and Mike Morrell, *The Divine Dance* (New Kensington, PA.: Whitaker House, 2016), 166.

61 Schofield, Stephen. ed., *In Search of C. S. Lewis* (South Plainfield, NJ: Bridge Publishing Inc., 1983), 53.

time England had ever known, they were in a place where laughter could still be heard.

I often buy a book for the subtitle. Matthew Paul Turner's *The Christian Culture* has the intriguing subtitle: *Survival Guide: The Misadventures of an Outsider on the Inside.* This is the kind of book that invites words you will find repeated in this book: reflection, re-evaluation, meditation, contemplation. A big seller for me was this line in the Preface: (And remember, this is meant to be a piece of humor!):

> If you have no sense of humor, please put this book back on the shelf, coffee table…where you found it and immediately read something written by Max Lucado, Chuck Swindoll, or the Pope. You'll feel better about yourself in the morning.
>
> (A page later): If those of you with no sense of humor are still reading: Yes, I do passionately love Jesus and look forward to spending eternity with him and most of you.[62]

In negotiating for a workshop or other speaking engagement, I always throw in somewhere: "I need to warn you I use a lot of humor – none of it crude, put-down, or inappropriate. But if you don't enjoy a good laugh now and then, you don't want me." I could add, but don't: "The only individuals or groups I have ever had any real problems with were those who had no sense of humor." In a serious world with serious problems and too many deadly serious people in charge, the last thing I need is to take myself (or even my situation) too seriously.

---

62 Turner, Matthew Paul. *The Christian Culture* (Lake Mary, FL: Relevant Books, 2004), xvii, xix.

QUESTIONS FOR REFLECTION, DISCOVERY, AND CONVERSATION

1. In what ways have you found humor/laughter to be beneficial?
2. Were you aware of how much laughter and humor there is in the Bible and in the teachings of Jesus?
3. Do you believe that appropriate humor lightens and enlivens everything?

How to Keep Meaning and Purpose in Your Life

Setting the Stage

Why is meaningless the calling card of our time?[63]

There is evidence that the search for meaning intensifies as we get older.[64]

Pursue What is Meaningful (Not What is Expedient)

The above is Rule Number 7 in Jordan B. Peterson's *12 Rules for Life.* Here is a brief excerpt about that rule:

> You may come to ask yourself, "What should I do today?" in a manner that means, "How could I use my time to make things better, instead of worse."
>
> There is no faith and no courage and no sacrifice in doing what is expedient.... To have meaning in your life is better than to have what you want, because you may neither know what you want, nor what you truly need. Meaning is something that comes upon you, of its own accord.

63 Wells, David F. *The Courage To Be Protestant* (Grand Rapids: William B. Eerdmans, 2008), 105.

64 Seymour, Robert E. *Aging Without Apology* (Valley Forge: Judson Press, 1995), 39.

Meaning is the Way, the path of life more abundant, the place you live when you are guided by Love and speaking Truth and when nothing you want or could possibly want takes any precedence over precisely that.

Do what is meaningful, not what is expedient.[65]

Even in our senior years, we continue to seek something that lifts us out of a world of self-centeredness and instant gratification. The meaning we seek has everything to do with things that are high and noble – things that make our lives matter. The subtitle of Peterson's book is *An Antidote to Chaos.* Released in a year in which chaos and confusion seemed to be the only game in town, it offers the prescription to do something other than rant and rave against so much that doesn't make sense.

Norman Doidge in the Forward writes: "These really are rules. And the foremost rule is that you must take responsibility for your own life. Period."[66] When I think about how difficult that is while one battles the assaults of aging, I am reminded of Victor Frankl's *Man's Search for Meaning.* How that search was even possible in a Nazi death camp is beyond my grasp. What Frankl writes is a challenge to me every day that I want to bemoan the difficulties of the "eighties" with which I have to contend.

Most men in a concentration camp believed that the real opportunities of life had passed. Yet, in reality, there was an opportunity and a challenge. One could make a victory of those experiences, turning life into an inner triumph, or one could ignore the challenge and simply vegetate, as did a majority of the prisoners.

We had to learn ourselves and, furthermore, we had to teach the despairing men, that it did not really matter what we expected from life, but rather what life expected from us. We needed to stop asking about the meaning of life, and instead to think of ourselves as those who were being questioned by

---

65   Peterson, Jordan B. *12 Rules for Life* (Toronto: Random House Canada, 2018), 199-201.

66   Ibid., xxiii.

life – daily and hourly. Our answer must consist, not in talk and meditation, but in right action and right conduct.

These tasks, and therefore the meaning of life, differ from man to man, and from moment to moment. Thus, it is impossible to define the meaning of life in a general way. Questions about the meaning of life can never be answered by sweeping statements.[67]

MEANING AND PURPOSE ARE UNIQUE TO EACH INDIVIDUAL

You don't have to be in a concentration camp to know that meaning and purpose vary greatly from person to person. It is impossible for me to tell another person how to have meaning in his/her life. Meaning is much like happiness. It is never found by directly pursuing it – it is always a by-product. "The pursuit of happiness" may be a guaranteed "right" but such pursuit is not a possibility. It comes to us because we are doing something else, usually in pursuit of a larger good than ourselves.

Helen Keller set the standard for me: "I long to accomplish a great and noble task, but it is my chief duty to accomplish small tasks as if they were great and noble."[68] That parallels Mother Teresa's, "We are not called to do great things. We are called to do small things with great love." With aging comes a diminishment in our dreams of doing the magnificent and the awe inspiring. Most of the time we are simply asking, "How can I make a small difference in someone's life?" In my research for this book, many of my sources related similar stories of those who began their day by determining to encourage all they met that day with cheerful, affirming, and encouraging words. In the nursing home, that meant the person who came to clean their room, the person who assisted in personal hygiene, the nurse who checked blood pressure and gave injections, the person who brought the meals, etc. Those who made this their mission always related that they felt so good at the end of the day.

67 Frankl, Viktor E. *Man's Search for Meaning*. (Boston: Beacon Press, 1959), 76.
68 Peck, M. Scott. *An Anthology of Wisdom*, 342.

Even if it's done imperfectly it can still be a blessing! I simply can't resist using this illustration:

> Once on a airplane, Fred Rogers was sitting in his blazer and his bow tie when a flight attendant came over and tapped him on the shoulder and said, "I don't mean to disturb you, but I just wanted to tell you how much I like your popcorn." She thought he was Orville Redenbacher. "For somebody that is recognized all the time, he just thought it was wonderful to be recognized as somebody else. He never tired of telling that one," (son) Jim Rogers remembers.[69]

A THEME THAT WILL KEEP COMING BACK

In writing about life in a monastery, Paul Wilkes observes: "Crucial to the foundation of the monastic approach to work is the approach we take to that work. The upshot of this is that primary value is not placed on the results of our efforts…but our intention, or attitude, or desire."[70] The results of our efforts are outside of our control – intention, attitude, and desire are not. As long as these are in place, the only things we can really be responsible for are taken care of. If someone we try to affirm and encourage doesn't respond with anything close to gratitude, what difference does it make? We have done what we felt was our calling for that day.

Having a purpose each day does not have to be something seen as significant by anyone else. As long as it's our purpose, we can make it significant. Brother Lawrence never did anything more significant in the monastery than what we would call KP. However, he maintained that he washed pots and pans for the glory of God. This quiet and unassuming saint surprised all who knew him by leaving a unique legacy. When he died, his brothers discovered a journal with prayers and meditations that has become one of the great devotional classics. Sidebar: Even if he had never written

---

69   King, Maxwell. *The Good Neighbor*, 300-301.
70   Wilkes, Paul. *Beyond the Walls* (New York: Image Books, 1999), 187.

what became a classic, his example of kitchen duty for the glory of God is worth remembering – and emulating!

Jonas Mekas is one of the six seniors John Leland spent a year interviewing for a book he ultimately titled *Happiness is a Choice You Make.* Jonas was ninety-two and reading about him is both challenging and inspiring:

> He often spoke about having angels to protect him, even claiming he had photographic proof of their existence....Angels protected him because he still had something to do...."Since I don't know why the angels saved us, to do what, I don't think about what I have to do, I just do it, hoping that that's what my fate is....Trust – that's what I advise if anyone asks. You have to trust your angels."

> His primary lesson is to maintain a purpose in life. The unspoken corollary, of course, is to find a purpose in the first place – starting now.[71]

What About When Things Get Really Limited

Most of us have a real dread of going to what used to be called a "nursing home." In the course of my ministry I have visited far too many and seen far too many unhappy, lonely people. To this day, I still see the large sitting rooms where wheel chairs are situated in front a television set tuned to anything that "passes the time." In another section, a bingo game is in progress. Many "inmates" (that is what too many people told me they felt like) simply remain in their rooms. Much is done to provide entertainment and something to while away the time.

Atul Gawande in his 2014 book *Being Mortal* gives this stark appraisal: "The waning days of our lives...are spent in institutions...where regimented, anonymous routines cut us off from all the things that matter to us in life."[72]

---

71 Leland, John. *Happiness is a Choice You Make*, 207-208.
72 Gawande, Atul. *Being Mortal,* 9.

Gawande's surprising and common sense suggestion should be required reading for all seniors and, absolutely, all care-givers. He maintains that most of the activities in such institutions are the result of family and staff ideas. His suggestion: Why not ask the patients what they would like to do? He began doing that for his study and the results brought about many changes in assisted-living facilities. I trust this one example will whet your appetite for reading the book:

> You don't ask, "What do you want when you are dying?" You ask, "If time becomes short, what is most important to you?"
> This totally shocked me: "Well, if I'm able to eat chocolate ice cream and watch football on TV then I'm willing to stay alive. I'm willing to go through a lot of pain if I have a shot at that."[73]

Sometimes it all boils down to asking, "Do I have a reason to get out of bed this morning?" (Assuming you are still able to do so.) Asking people what would bring some meaning and purpose to their lives is always the question to ask. I, for one, certainly do not want to watch TV and play bingo all the remaining days of my life. It will also take more than chocolate ice cream and a football game but, then again, if I'm in the situation of the man Gawande quotes, it might be something pretty close.

The bottom line is that meaning and purpose are a must at every age but definitely when we are older. These quotes from *Happiness is a Choice You Make* tell us just how important that is:

> Patricia Boyle, researcher at the Rush Alzheimer's disease Center in Chicago: "Having a purpose creates a 'reserve' that enables some brains to form other pathways to transmit signals and nutrients and remain functional. The stronger the purpose, the more protective it is.
> Researchers have long observed that older people who feel a sense of purpose in their lives tend to live longer, fuller, and healthier lives than people who don't.

73 Ibid, 182, 183.

As in previous studies, people who had a purpose in life suffered less memory loss over the eight years of the study than those who didn't.[74]

QUESTIONS FOR REFLECTION, DISCOVERY, AND CONVERSATION

1. With the increasing years, how have you attempted to keep meaning in your life?
2. What do you see as the value of placing effort, intention, and desire over results?
3. What are your reasons for getting up each day?

---

74 Leland, John. *Happiness is a Choice You Make*, 203, 204.

CHAPTER 7

PRACTICE DAILY THE PAUSE THAT REFRESHES

SETTING THE STAGE

"If I were a doctor and asked for my advice, I would reply, Create Silence." Soren Kierkegaard.[75]

"May we all grow in grace and peace, and not neglect the silence that is printed in the center of our being. It will not fail us." Thomas Merton.[76]

The capacity to reflect and recognize rather than recall and remember increase until 60; they can often be the same at age 80 as age 30.[77]

THE FOOTBALL ENJOINER THAT HAS BECOME THE NATIONAL SLOGAN

It was the first time in many years my wife and I had attended a university football game. Having been priced out of the market, we became regular members of the TV audience. Then some friends

---

75 Buford, Bob. *Half Time* (Grand Rapids: Zondervan, 2008), 66.
76 Arrien, Angeles. *The Second Half of Life,* 156.
77 Valliant, George E. *Aging Well* (Boston: Little Brown and Company, 2001), 238.

had a couple of spare tickets to a Louisville football game and we gladly accepted their offer. It turned out to be a great day except for one ingredient I had missed as a TV watcher.

The cheerleaders never seemed to be satisfied with the level of participation of those in the stands because the message that kept flashing throughout the game on the message boards was "GET LOUDER." I'm not certain how many decibels they were after, but I now have a new appreciation for just how loud things can get: much too loud!

If your experience is like mine, there is no place you can go (doctors' offices at the top of the list) where there is not a TV turned to a level that is guaranteed to make conversation and reading difficult. The music level in restaurants is usually just shy of making conversation impossible. (Sidebar: Once when my wife politely asked the manager if he could turn down the volume, he replied, "We keep it at that level to keep the staff on their toes." I had several replies I wanted to make, none of which seemed to be suitable for public consumption.)

Noise pollution has often been called the number one pollution problem in the culture. (Let's not even talk about the sound level of movies where even the seats vibrate.) For those who shake their heads at the "elevator music" of my generation, I would simply like to say that it was definitely *background* music as opposed to the stage center bombardments of the current public places. When did silence become such a national sin?

KIERKEGAARD AND MERTON ARE RIGHT!

One of the encouraging signs I have seen is the addition of a period of silence that some school systems have adopted for their elementary classes. The results? Attention, participation, and test scores improve. Except in private religious schools, this is not a specifically "religious" experience. It is simply a time to be quiet and become centered and focused. It is a brief time to shut out the distractions and cacophony of a world with seemingly no control button for the volume level of anything.

This chapter's title comes from the Coca Cola marketing slogan of some years ago. There is no doubt that the break in one's routine, plus the caffeine and sugar, provided a pause that prepared for re-entry into the work day. While most of us do begin our day with a cup (several?) of coffee or tea, the pause I am suggesting is one that will refresh our minds, hearts, and spirits and prepare us to enter into the day with a perspective and disposition much better suited for facing our worlds of serendipity. I call it the pause that changes everything.

I try to begin my day with a thirty-minute period of devotional and Scripture reading, meditation, and prayer. For years I have been using the three volume set *The Divine Hours* edited by Phyllis Tickle. The subtitle is *A Manual for Prayer* and each day has a brief section of biblical selections and prayers. I always use those for the morning and, occasionally, those for other portions of the day. (There is one for the Morning Office, the Midday Office, the Vespers Office, and the Night Office.) When I am able to read these selections out loud, they have been more beneficial. There is something to hearing your own voice read the Scripture and offer the prayers that makes them come alive.

The concluding prayer for ~~each day~~ the Morning is always the same:

Lord God, almighty and everlasting Father, you have brought me in safety to this new day. Preserve me with your mighty power, that I may not fall into sin, nor be overcome by adversity; and in all I do direct me to the fulfilling of your purpose; through Jesus Christ my Lord. Amen.[78]

If you feel you don't have thirty minutes, begin with at least ten minutes in total silence with no distractions. Regardless of what finds its way into your day, closing the day with an equal

---

78 Tickle, Phyllis. *The Divine Hours* (New York: Doubleday, 2001).

period of quiet gives two bookends for keeping life in something like day-tight compartments. It also reminds us that each day is a gift and that, contrary to Scarlett O'Hara's philosophy, tomorrow may *not* be another day.

It's a Common Dis-ease

Although this is an extreme case, all of us can see something of ourselves in the way a psychiatrist describes one of his patients:

> She had no self. She was, instead, a walking cacophony of unintegrated experiences.
>
> Miss S knew nothing about herself. She knew nothing about other individuals. She knew nothing about her world. She was a movie played out of focus.[79]

The pause that refreshes always includes time for reflection either on what you believe is coming in your day or each night as a time for assessing just what happened during the day. When people tell me they don't know how to pray, I always give them a simple way to start. In the morning, tell the Lord how you are feeling about the things you believe are going to be coming your way – your dreams, hopes, anxieties, and fears. At the end of the day, imagine God asking you, "Well, how did things go?" And then honestly respond to that question.

All of us have heard that "the unexamined life is not worth living." I would add: "The life without reflection is hardly lived." In my reading, I find more than one writer lamenting: "It's here, in reflection, where our culture is perhaps at its weakest relative to the ancients."[80] For the ancients, reflection was simply a part of life. Travel meant walking. "Without radio or phones or the internet, you were alone with your thoughts – one foot in front of the other, mile after mile."[81] Most of us cannot imagine what it would be like to have large chunks of time during each day in which you had

79 Peterson, Jordan B. *12 Rules For Life,* 235-236.
80 Greitens, Eric. *Resilience,* 194.
81 Ibid, 195.

time to reflect on what you were experiencing. Life would not a series of "happenings," it would be a series of experiences.

How Is Your EQ?

I vividly remember having an IQ test when I was a high school student and having a classmate quietly announce to me, "I saw your score. You're just average." My response: "Well, I guess I'll just have to work harder." And I have. Probably I would be labeled an "over-achiever" but that's okay with me. In my later years, I have realized how little IQ has to do with what we accomplish in life or what we become. (Much more on this in a later chapter). My real weakness was in the area of EQ – Emotional Quotient.

> Emotions are a language that speak to us of the deeper workings of our mind and if listened to – rather than reacted to – can provide valuable insights into ourselves, our children, loved ones and friends. Yet, in themselves, emotions are not a proper destination point. They are a door that must be seen but also must be opened...Surprisingly few people take time to identify the thoughts behind their emotions....Your EQ is more important than your IQ.[81]

It should come as no surprise that:

> Effective emotional knowledge demands a profound level of self-reflection, an active imagination, and an ability not only to envision alternative approaches to a given situation but also to understand that there are entire invisible galaxies of salient emotional facts behind almost every workplace exchange.[82]

In the margin beside that paragraph I wrote: "Same for church!" I could have added: "And the family." If you think congregations leave their experiences, problems, difficulties, emotions, humanity, and basic personalities at the sanctuary door, you just need to work closely with church committees for a while. This is not a negative statement; it is the recognition of the many "emo-

---

82 Prather, Hugh. *The Little Book of Letting Go*, 54-55.

tional facts" that are a part of every discussion, every interaction, every meeting you are a part of. That's one of the reasons maintaining healthy relationships does not come easily

To reflect on why I feel the way I do, why certain people bother me just by showing up, why I react the way I do, etc. are all reasons self-reflection is so necessary and yet so difficult. Attempting to understand myself helps me understand why it is so difficult to understand others. At times we all feel like the demented man in the gospel story who, when asked his name, gave a number: legion (Mark 5:9; Luke 8:30). The term refers to a group of Roman soldiers numbering from 3,000 to 6,000. I have never felt quite that divided but I understand what it means to feel that there are a lot of different and competing emotions going on within me. We are much more complex than we usually recognize – and so is everyone else. It is in continuing reflection that we begin to unravel some of that complexity.

LET'S ALSO INCLUDE MEDITATION

Meditation refers to a directed time for reflection in which Bible verses, key devotional phrases, or single words can become the focus for an extended period of time. Most of us do not find this to be very easy and it takes real effort to keep the mind from wandering. I suppose I prefer the term contemplation which I find more easily achieved. Contemplation is always a part of my morning devotional and meditation time.

Most of us have an agenda (even as the years increase) and usually begin the day with a "must do" list. Donald Altman in his book *Clearing Emotional Clutter* writes an entire chapter on one of the major difficulties in doing this: "Put The Brakes on Work and Speed." He writes:

> The irony is that the more we try to do and the more transitions we navigate, the less time we have for deeper exploration. We multitask at work and are actually less productive.

Our busy lives leave little time for long, meaningful, uninterrupted face-to-face time with family and friends.

Instead of swimming in the deep mysteries of the ocean,
we wade in the shallows of the pool.[83]

One of the positives that aging brings us is that we don't have
to pack our days full of activity and we don't have to feel guilty
about not "making every minute count" (whatever that means!).
With all the devices we have purchased to make life easier and
paper-free, we find ourselves busier than ever and buying paper by
the carton. Even the church has succumbed to the speed "demon"
and the emphasis on maximum effort during every minute of the
day. The author of *Introverts in the Church* was being interviewed
for the associate pastor position in a church of 300 members. Here
is what the pastor told him:

> "This is really a high-octane environment. We're looking
> for someone who is excitable and high energy. You have to be
> totally sold out to work here. We work at full throttle." The
> author writes: "I double-checked my surroundings to make
> certain I was at a church and hadn't stumbled into an interview
> for the pit crew at the Indianapolis Speedway."[84]

It seems to me that the deep things of life, the deep things of
the Spirit, the deep things of the soul are what those of us in our
eighties are after. I was blessed in my seminary career to come
in contact with professors who were into those deep things and
taught those of us who were their students the value and necessity
of slowing down for the pause that not only refreshes but redirects
us to the detours and lay-bys that make the journey meaningful
and truly productive. I am grateful that no congregation ever de-
manded that I live at full-throttle. I am grateful that my present life
can be structured so that with prayer, meditation, and reflection I
can discover and give myself to the things in life that really matter.

---

83 Altma, Donald. *Clearing Emotional Clutter* (New York: MJF Books,
    2016), 140.

84 McHugh, Adam S. *Introverts in the Church* (Downers Grove IL: IVP
    Books, 2009), 26.

QUESTIONS FOR REFLECTION, DISCOVERY, AND CONVERSATION

1. Do you have a regular time each day for silence, meditation, and prayer? In what ways might it be modified or expanded?

2. Are you aware of the many times Jesus withdrew from the crowd (and even from his disciples) for times of quiet, meditation, and prayer (even many all night sessions)? Do you think this had anything to do with his effectiveness?

3. How would you rate your EQ? How might it be improved?

LIVE GRATEFULLY AND
CELEBRATE EVERYTHING

SETTING THE STAGE

> Cicero called gratitude "not only the greatest of
> virtues, but the parent of all the others."[85]

> From a 2015 project at the University of Southern
> California to study what happens in the brain of
> a person feeling gratitude: The more grateful that
> subjects said they were, the stronger the response
> in the regions of their brains governing moral and
> social cognition.[86]

> The title of Huston Smith's And Live Rejoicing is
> based on a line from the Gospel song, "Oh, Hap-
> py Day." The book was released in 2012 when
> Smith was about 94 years old. He has truly "lived
> rejoicing" all of his life and he says that his secret is
> that he has lived with gratitude.[87]

---

85 Leland, John. Happiness is a Choice You Make, 118.
86 Ibid, 119.
87 Smith, Huston. *And Live Rejoicing* (Novato: New World Library, 2012),
    xiii-xiv.

Have We Lost the Simple "Thank You"?

I confess that a part of my daily newspaper reading always includes "Dear Annie," the successor to the long-running Ann Landers advice column. Most of the problems presented by readers are rooted in relationships. A frequent generational complaint comes from grandparents who recognize important days in the lives of their grandchildren but never receive a thank you note. I have heard too many explain that people no longer write notes but send text messages. Emily Post is no longer with us but good manners always include a response to a gift and I maintain that nothing takes the place of a brief handwritten note.

There is no shortage of current books challenging the value of texting and emails as effective communication. Nothing takes the place of face to face conversation for genuine communication and nothing takes the place of a written note (and even a letter!) for the truly personal touch. It almost makes you weep to see a family having dinner at a restaurant with each member glued to a screen. I witnessed such a scene in which the family members never made eye contact with one another. Those of us who are seniors can and must set a better example as we attempt to connect with those of the younger generation. (Speechless was my only response when I saw a two year old with her "beginners" computer – using it with ability and great delight.)

Moderation in all things is still some of the best advice I have ever been given. Except there are some things that need to be excessive. Take this example:

> G. K. Chesterton wrote that "thanks are the highest form of thought, and…gratitude is happiness doubled by wonder," and made a habit of saying grace not just before meals, but "before the play and the opera, and grace before the concert and the pantomime, and grace before I open a book, and grace be-

fore sketching, painting, swimming, fencing, boxing, walking, playing, dancing and grace before I dip the pen in the ink."[88]

We shouldn't wait until the later years in life to discover that everything is a gift. Once this becomes our basic attitude, gratitude also becomes a daily habit.

And "gratitude becomes happiness doubled by wonder." From a lost source, here is a quote I can now appreciate: "At the age of eighty-eight Ludwig Von Mises (an Austrian economist) was asked how he felt upon getting up in the morning. He replied, 'Amazed.'" Wonder, amazement, gift! There is only one possible response to such a discovery: Meister Eckhart said that if the only prayer you ever pray is "thank you" then you have prayed well enough.[89]

THE MORE YOU ARE GRATEFUL THE MORE YOU FIND TO BE GRATEFUL FOR

David Steindl-Rast, author of *Gratefulness, The Heart of Prayer,* writes: "As I express my gratitude, I become more deeply aware of it."[90] But what if life is so limited, so unpleasant, so full of misery and woe that there is nothing you could possibly be grateful for? Victor Frankl addresses that situation set in a concentration camp in *Man's Search for Meaning:*

> We were grateful for the smallest of mercies. We were glad when there was time to delouse before going to bed, although in itself this was no pleasure, as it meant standing naked in an unheated hut where icicles hung from the ceiling. But we were thankful if there was no air raid alarm during this operation and the lights were not switched off. If we could not do the job properly, we were kept awake half the night.[91]

---

88 Leland, John. *Happiness is a Choice*, 118.
89 Willimon, William H. *Sinning Like A Christian* (Nashville: Abingdon, **2005), 105.**
90 Creagan, Edward T. ed., *Mayo Clinic on Healthy Aging*, 87.
91 Frankl, Viktor E. *Man's Search For Meaning*, 46.

I often think of how many people would be grateful for the daily necessities of life that I take for granted. That's where my gratitude list begins each day.

> If we shift as we age toward appreciating everyday plea-
> sures and relationships rather than toward achieving, having,
> and getting, and if we find this more fulfilling, then why do we
> take so long to do it? Why do we wait until we're old?...What
> if the change in needs and desires has nothing to do with age
> per se? Suppose it merely has to do with perspective – your
> personal sense of how finite your time in this world is.[92]

The things we value in old age are the very things we should have been valuing at every age.

Along With That Gratitude Comes Celebration

An anonymous fifty-five year old poet in addressing the difference between successful and unsuccessful aging wrote, "One, I guess you would call 'the celebrant sense' or that wonderful hippie word, 'Wow!'...Life needs to be enjoyed!"[93] Most of our lives are too short on celebration and too long on complaining. It's the easiest thing to do and there is always something to complain about! There is also always something to celebrate if we can get out of what someone has called the "kickative" mode of living. There is never a shortage of things to kick and rant and rave about. It has almost become our national pastime. But have you noticed the hunger for genuine celebration and reasons to shout "Wow!"? All we need to do is keep the "celebrant sense" alive.

As I write this, Christmas was just a few days ago and the unwrapping of gifts was one of the great delights of Christmas morning. The anticipation just kept growing as we daily eyed the packages under the tree. There is still that child in all of us. Ruth Ann Schabacker maintains: "Each day comes bearing gifts. Untie

---

92 Gawande, Atul. *Being Mortal,* 248.
93 Vaillan, George. *Aging Well,* 15.

the ribbons."[94] The gifts that life has to offer are not confined to a few special days in the year. Too many of them come unrecognized because they are not available on-line or at the mall. "Untie the ribbons" means "Take the gift out of the box." There are many ways to untie the ribbons of life's gifts and I trust you have discovered some of those ways. I continue to believe that the most impossible thing in the world is to "cheer up" somebody who doesn't want to be cheered up! The corollary is that I don't believe it's possible to untie for someone else the ribbons on life's gifts. It's strictly a do it yourself project.

> People who age successfully spend a lifetime appreciating and enjoying the little, simple pleasures other people overlook – a beautify flower, a walk in the woods, or the sound of the birds singing in the early morning. The ability to experience pleasure is a hallmark of successful aging.[95]

A popular song of days gone by (where so many of my favorite songs have gone) was titled "Little Things Mean A Lot." They can and they do when we take the time to notice. The list is not the same for all of us and there is no prescribed formula for "you must enjoy these things." Find those little things that mean a lot to you and celebrate them.

Book titles fascinate me and are often the reason for the purchase. *Cleaning Emotional Clutter* has already been mentioned and the title caused me to pick up the book. The chapters further intrigued me, especially the one titled "Take Daily Snapshots of Joy." In it the author related his experience of conducting a workshop on his book *Living Kindness* and asking the group of about twenty-five: "How many of you have felt gratitude for something in your life already today?" It was just a little past noon. Not a single hand went up![96]

---

94   Wolfelt, Alan D. & Kirby J. Duvall, *Healing Your Grief About Aging*, 68.
95   O'Brien, Mary. *Successful Aging*, 12.
96   Altman, Donald. *Clearing Emotional Clutter*, 205-206.

My advice: to keep gratitude and celebration alive in your life, always be ready to take daily snapshots of joy. And be sure you share those snapshots with others.

QUESTIONS FOR REFLECTION, DISCOVERY, AND CONVERSATION

1. Why is gratitude so basic to all the other virtues?
2. How have you learned to untie the ribbons of the gifts that each day brings?
3. Have you found with getting older that "Little Things Mean A Lot"? Name some of those little things that now mean more to you.

EXERCISE YOUR BODY AND YOUR MIND

SETTING THE STAGE

Exercise is probably the single most important thing you can do to age successfully.[97]

The bottom line is that the aging brain is far more capable and resilient than we used to think.[98]

IT'S NUMBER ONE IN EVERY BOOK ON AGING I HAVE EVER READ

"Keep moving" is always the first piece of advice I have found in every book on successful aging. Becoming a "couch potato" at any point in life is the recipe for physical, mental, and emotional decline. Inactivity is the recipe for more inactivity. On both sides, my grandparents were farmers. Getting up before the chickens was the required way of life and, because there was always something to do, most never had to take a sleep aid at night. Their diets may not have been the healthiest (I still remember the fried chicken and fried pies!) but perhaps some of that was offset by a very active

---

97   Creagan, Edward T. ed., *Mayo Clinic on Healthy Aging*, 13
98   Wolfelt, Alan D. & Kirby J. Duvall, *Healing Your Grief About Aging*, 29.

lifestyle. The major negative was the lack of periodic and on-going healthcare. A visit to or from the doctor meant something serious had developed.

We now must deliberately plan some sort of daily exercise. Five to seven days a week I ride an exercise bike for at least thirty minutes. Household chores (one of things for men that retirement brings) keep me moving most mornings. "Take two squirrels and call me in the morning" is a prescription from a doctor who wants his patients to get outside as much as possible.[99] Walking, even at a leisurely pace, has proven to have beneficial effects. One of those benefits is an improvement in mood and attitude. "I just feel so much better when I get my daily walk," is the consistent testimony from most of the seniors I know.

The exercise business has become big business due to the sedentary crisis in the culture and the repeated admonitions from the medical community. Senior rates are always available and joining some sort of a program with a friend is a good way to make exercise a regular part of your life. Limiting the amount of screen time in one's life is essential for "finding the time" for the truly essential. In 1985 Neil Postman wrote his now largely unheard of *Amusing Ourselves to Death: Public Discourse in the Age of Show Business*. In the 2005 edition, his son Andrew Postman wrote a new introduction in which he notes that the number of hours the average American watches TV has remained steady, at about four and a half hours a day, every day. "By the age sixty-five, a person will have spent twelve uninterrupted years in front of the TV. Childhood obesity is way up."[100] I have read current estimates that raise the total number of all types of screen time to as much as six or seven hours a day.

---

99 Finkelstein, Michael. *77 Questions for Skillful Living* (New York: William Morrow, 2013), 93.
100 Postman, Neil. *Amusing Ourselves to Death* (New York: Penguin Books, 2005), xiv.

The new introduction to Postman's book also has an interesting observation on how screen time robs us of opportunities to exercise our minds. A student named Jonathan made this observation:

> "In the book (Postman) makes the point that there is no reflection time in the world anymore. When I go to a restaurant, everyone's on their cell phone, talking or playing games. I have no ability to sit by myself and just think."[101]

Since 2005, the number of new cable channels and the new sources for streaming have made the choices for viewing unlimited. Andrew commends his father for asking such good questions in his book. "His questions can be asked about all technologies and media. What happens to us when we become infatuated with and then seduced by them? Do they free us or imprison us?"[102] I love a good movie. I love good entertainment – but not as the staff of life, not as the core of my existence, not as the shaper of my hopes and dreams, not as the thing to which I will devote most of my waking hours. Media can give us many things but in excess it can rob us of the very things that make life, especially in our later years, healthy and productive.

You Can Teach an Old Dog New Tricks

The above heading is a reversal of the piece of folk wisdom that has become accepted as one of life's rules. Like so much of what we have heard all our lives, it needs to be re-examined in the light of examples from history and present day realities. All of us have been inspired by stories of those who have made some of their greatest contributions in their eighties and nineties. These examples usually come from famous people who might be seen as exceptional. In my almost six decades of ministry I have been impressed by the "ordinary" people who have made extraordinary, if unheralded, accomplishments.

---

101 Ibid, x.
102 Ibid, xv.

Perhaps the examples of senior accomplishments we have seen celebrated have, instead of motivating us, discouraged us because they have made our talents seem too small to matter. Do I have to paint like Winston Churchill or Grandma Moses in order to pick up a brush and splash the colors on a canvas? I was once asked if I had ever done any painting. When asked if they could see some of my work, I replied, "It's all what I call 'attic art.' It's not exhibition painting." One day, who knows?

Why not take up something you have not done before? Why not learn a new language, begin a new hobby, learn to play the piano, take a university extension course, explore a field you know absolutely nothing about? Why not expand your horizons, your perspectives, your knowledge, your skills? You are not set in stone, regardless of your age. In *The New York Review of Books* I saw a brief review of a book labeled "for life-long learners": *Make It Stick: The Science of Successful Learning* by Peter C. Brown, Henry L. Roediger III, and Mark A. McDaniel. The complaint most of us make is, "I just can't remember things like I used to." We usually are referring to some specific piece of information, a fact of some sort. Does that mean we cannot learn anything new? (And is just the recall of information what knowledge and wisdom are all about?)

The practical and doable techniques I found In *Make It Stick* I can readily apply to my life at eighty-four as well as I could have done at twenty-four. The authors do give some concessions that need to be made for people of my age. There is the account of pianist Thelma Hunter who won her first prize as a pianist at age five in New York and at eighty-eight continues to perform.

> But Hunter has made some concessions to age. She never used to warm up before playing, but now she does. "My stamina is not as great as it used to be. My reach is not as big. Now, if I memorize something, I have to think about it. I never used to have to do that, I just worked through all the aspects

of it and the memorizing came." She visualizes the score and makes mental marginalia. [103]

At the writing of the book, Hunter was learning four *new* works for an upcoming concert performance: pieces by Mozart, Faure, Rachmaninoff, and William Bolcom. If you will permit me to say it, she was learning "new tricks" at eighty-eight.

Have Any Good Books Read You Lately?

The above is not a typo. You have often heard someone say, "I don't read the Bible; it reads me." That is true of so many of the books I have read. They cause me to explore, to question, to re-examine, and to re-think so that I will not succumb to the oft-quoted line from an old radio show, *The Life of Riley*, where the star would often say, "My head is made up." It's the "I shall not be moved" in more earthy language. We are told that the brain is much more pliable than we used to think (except, of course, in the case of some people I have known where it appears to have ossified years ago). To keep it pliable I have to continue to allow new synapses to form by introducing new ideas and new patterns into my thinking and my routines. New connections do not appear to be made if we continue to use the old avenues of thought.

Reading Neil Postman reminded me of a comparison I had seen before. George Orwell in *1984* feared that books would be banned. Aldous Huxley in *Brave New World* feared there would be no one who wanted to read one. Postman then gives this insight from Richard Hofstadter:

> America was founded by intellectuals, a rare occurrence in the history of modern nations. "The Founding Fathers," he writes, "were sages, scientists, men of broad cultivation, many of them apt in classical learning, who used their wide reading

---

103 Brown, Peter C., Henry L. Roediger III, and Mark A. McDaniel, *Make it Stick* (Cambridge: The Belknap Press, 2014), 224.

in history, politics, and law to solve the exigent problems of their time." [104]

My gratitude continues to expand for the contribution my parents and my teachers made to my education: the love of reading. My father was an avid reader and my most vivid recollection of him is in his "easy chair" reading. When I was still a preschooler my mother took me to the local library for "story time" and to help me select books for "picture reading." My teachers, particularly those in my seminary and graduate years, taught me how to be a life-long learner through continued reading. I once had a member of my congregation tease me by saying that if I didn't have anything else to read, I would probably read soup labels. She was right.

Through the years too many have told me they simply did not enjoy reading. My advice was to find something for a fun read. That's where I began as a boy. As an adult I have tried to continue the practice recommended to me: I try to keep at least five books going. I always read the Scriptures, a devotional (inspirational) book of some kind, a book on some aspect of biblical theology, a book of general knowledge of some sort, a book I know I ought to be reading, and a mystery. The mystery is my late night reading, just for fun reading (nothing serious to keep my mind churning). My current mystery is an old Erle Stanley Gardner mystery: *The D. A. Calls It Murder.* I can't resist the Half Price bookstores in Louisville. (I got hooked during my year in Austin, Texas, when I discovered their flagship store.) I also receive Daedalus catalogues that give me access to bargain books in many fields. Barnes and Noble and Carmichael's book stores are also included in my book searching. I don't rush my reading and it doesn't matter how long it takes to finish a particular book.

Do I remember everything I read? No, but I read with pencil in hand and mark the significant things I find. Later, I type important references and quotes, put a copy in the book, and put another in my "information" file which is used for sermon illustra-

---

104 Postman, Neil. *Amusing Ourselves to Death*, 41.

tions and in writing. I'm not trying to overwhelm you with this suggestion but if you had to give a weekly sermon (when I began I had to preach twice every Sunday!), lead Bible studies, and give workshops you had better be a wide and active reader. Fortunately, I love what I do. It is my passion. Find what you love to do, what your passion is, and don't put your mind and your life into neutral just because aging makes some things more difficult. Difficult doesn't mean impossible.

EXERCISING YOUR MIND MEANS LIFELONG LEARNING

Lifelong learning makes the difference between healthy and unhealthy aging....The problem with aging is not age, it is petrifaction, rigidity of soul, inflexibility. Only ideas keep ideas flowing.[105]

Several years ago I heard Joan Chittister at a workshop in Austin, Texas. Two other outstanding speakers, both men, were on the program. If this had been a contest, she would have won it hands down. She is a prolific writer and if you want a good book on spirituality, you can't miss with one of hers.

Aging is not enough in itself. Aging well is the real goal of life. To allow ourselves to age without vitality, without energy, without purpose, without growth is simply to get old rather than to age well as we go.[106]

You don't have to get old! Chittister is right: to get old is to age without vitality, energy, purpose, or growth. Lifelong learning is a basic requirement to avoid petrifaction and rigidity of the soul. Too much is forgotten about the contribution of older persons who have not put their minds up on the shelf. "When companies run suggestion boxes, there is evidence that older employees tend to submit more ideas and high-quality ideas than their younger col-

---

105 Chittister, Joan. *The Gift of Years* (New York: BlueBridge, 2008), 98.
106 Ibid, 131.

leagues...." [107] I believe this is due in large measure to something
I urge you not to forget. The one thing that can increase in aging
is wisdom.

> On the "wisdom scale", Baltes (a researcher) found that
> older people did very well – more than half of the wisest re-
> sponses, came from subjects over age 60....In his nineties the
> great pianist Arthur Rubinstein was still playing concerts and
> when asked how he kept up such demanding activity, he cited
> three wise strategies: perform fewer pieces, practice each piece
> more frequently, and – to compensate for loss of speed and
> mental dexterity – slow down for a few seconds just before the
> music enters a particularly fast passage (your music will then
> sound faster than it really is!) [108]

Now that is wisdom! We just need to realize that old age does
not have to mean a decline in everything. Wisdom can increase
and so can our brains! "Improved MRI scanning has revealed that
contrary to decades of medical science, brains continue to develop
new neurons throughout life, and that people can increase their
number of brain cells the same way they build biceps, through regular exercise." [109] I had mentioned this idea earlier but just wanted
to let you know it is not wishful thinking. Exercising the body
and the mind has been scientifically proven to make a tremendous
amount of difference in the way we age. Aging is not an option;
but the way we handle it is. A bit of further proof on the lighter
side closes this section:

> John Gardner (former Secretary of Health, Education,
> and Welfare) once told me that he planned to learn and grow
> as much between ages seventy and eighty-eight as between zero
> and eighteen. When challenged, Gardner said that he knew a
> little more about learning at seventy that when he was zero. [110]

---

107 Grant, Adam. Originals: How Non-Conformists Move the World (New
    York: Viking, 2016), 109.
108 Chopra, Depak. *Ageless Body, Timeless Mind,* 248.
109 Leland, John. *Happiness is a Choice You Make,* 91.
110 Buford, Bob. *Half Time* (Grand Rapids, Zondervan, 2008), 15.

QUESTIONS FOR REFLECTION, DISCOVERY, AND CONVERSATION

1. Are you surprised that in every book on the requirements for healthy aging, exercise is at the top of the list?
2. Have any good books read you lately?
3. How have you avoided "petrifaction and rigidly of the soul"?

WHAT IF THE WORST HAPPENS?

SETTING THE STAGE

Changes In age-adjusted death rates in 2000 vs. 2010: Cancer: - 15%; Diabetes: -17.5%; Heart Disease: - 30.5%; Alzheimer's Disease: +39.4%[111]

As Alzheimer' disease progresses, brain tissue shrinks. As the ventricles enlarge and the cells of the shrinking hippocampus degenerate, memory declines. When the disease spreads throughout the cerebral cortex, language, judgment, behavior, and bodily functions decline along with memory until death, usually 8 to 10 years after diagnosis.[112]

A FEAR GREATER THAN DEATH

After listening to literally thousands of seniors and probing my own soul, I have concluded that Alzheimer's disease is feared more than death. Many have told me, "I would prefer to die rather than to be stricken with something that takes me away while I am still alive." As with so many things in life, we are not able to choose

---

111 Alzheimer's Disease Research, *A BrightFocus Foundation Program* (Clarksburg, MD, 2018).
112 Ibid.

which battles we will have to fight or what dark valleys we will have to walk through with those we love.

Only those who have confronted this unmerciful disease know the pain of looking into the face of someone we have known for years only to be met with an unknowing stare. As a pastor, visiting in the memory care units of assisted-living facilities has been the most difficult aspect of my ministry. To have a long-time member with whom I had developed a deep friendship look at me and say, "Now who did you say you were?" is painful beyond description.

As of this writing, there is no known cure for Alzheimer's. The alarming rise in its frequency is higher than the outdated statistic given at the top of the page. One of the factors in this statistic is the ability of the medical community to deal effectively with some conditions that were once fatal. Remember: we have not been able to increase the lifespan (which is now 85) but we have been able to increase life expectancy. The number 85 is the general rule of thumb and fluctuates due to many factors. Just this last week, the oldest living veteran of WWII died at the age of 112. And he did not have Alzheimer's.

In this section, I want to talk about some things we can do and mention some resources that are available for on-going assistance. Personal choices and decisions play a large role in how one faces this calamity. There is no concrete set of rules for effectiveness. There are only guidelines and general principles. Each situation is unique because we are each unique but there are some basics that should guide our decision making.

HELP AND RESOURCES ARE AVAILABLE

This has been the most difficult chapter to write because I have journeyed with far too many through this wilderness of help-lessness as they faced an incurable disease. Yet, through the years I have been inspired and humbled by the courage, commitment, and perseverance that have produced remarkable challenges to the total domination of this scourge. As long as life lasts, there is always something we can do rather than totally succumb to the role of victim.

My first rule of thumb is to not go it alone. There are too many groups and individuals with whom one can connect that provide resources for emotional and procedural support. If you are not familiar with any, the place to begin is to contact your local Alzheimer's Association. Often your doctor will give you a list of support groups. I have been amazed at the quality of life many have been able to maintain in spite of the impairments brought about by Alzheimer's.

I highly recommend the *Mayo Clinic Guide to Alzheimer's Disease*. It is an inexpensive and thorough guide to just about everything you need to know. In your personal reading, begin with this book. It is the most comprehensive guide I have found. Don't wait until you begin to detect symptoms in yourself (always difficult to do) or someone you love. We already know people who are dealing with Alzheimer's and this book will supply the necessary reliable information for a basic knowledge and understanding of the disease.

The Bright Focus Foundation funds Alzheimer's Disease Research and provides a wide variety of brochures on every aspect of the disease. I am on their mailing list and receive regular pamphlets that provide invaluable information. From a recent publication I was reminded:

> Alzheimer's disease is difficult to diagnose. It does not affect every patient in the same way. Alzheimer's disease usually progresses gradually, lasting from two to twenty years, with an average duration of seven years. The majority of Alzheimer's disease cases are late-onset (developing after age 60). Late-onset Alzheimer's has no known cause and shows no obvious inheritance pattern. Alzheimer's is a disease and should not be confused with old age or "senility." It is a degenerative disease of the brain and not a mental disorder. Physicians are not yet able to stop the progression of Alzheimer's disease or reverse

its damage to the brain. Caregivers can only strive to make patients' last months or years more calm and pleasant.

If you are a caregiver, having resources that provide responsible information and sharing regularly with others how you are doing physically and emotionally will assist you in taking care of yourself. The old cliché is correct: If you don't take care of yourself first you won't be able to take care of anyone else.

SOME OF THE EARLIEST SIGNS AND SYMPTOMS OF MILD STAGE ALZHEIMER'S

1. Not remembering recent events.
2. Asking the same questions repeatedly.
3. Getting lost in conversations and having problems finding the right word.
4. Not being able to complete familiar tasks, for example, someone who loves to cook having difficulties with a recipe.
5. Having problems with abstract thought, for example, uncertainty over using a credit card for financial transactions.
6. Misplacing items in inappropriate places, such as putting a watch, wallet or handbag in the refrigerator.
7. Undergoing sudden, intense changes in mood or behavior with no apparent reasons for the change.
8. ~~8.~~ ~~9.~~ Showing an inability to concentrate for more than a few minutes or to take initiative and complete projects.
9. ~~10.~~ Showing less interest in what's going on in the surroundings.
10. ~~11.~~ Showing an indifference toward personal appearance, for example, being unwashed, uncombed and poorly dressed.
11. ~~12.~~ Not observing normal courtesies to others, for example, ignoring greetings and simple questions.

(2 13. Feeling disoriented about time and place, for example, uncertainty about the general locations of stores in town.

13 14. Becoming lost while driving on familiar streets. [113]

The Mayo Clinic guide also lists the signs and symptoms of the moderate stage and gives information on what the doctor is looking for before the diagnosis of Alzheimer's is made.

Here are some of the things you will find in the 380 page *Mayo Clinic Guide to Alzheimer's Disease*:

AGING AND DEMENTIA: What is dementia? What to expect as you grow older. Diagnosing dementia.

ALZHEIMER'S DISEASE: The basics of Alzheimer's disease. Biological basis of Alzheimer's. Treatment of Alzheimer's.

NON-ALZHEIMER'S FORMS OF DEMENTIA: Frontotemporal dementia. Dementia with Lewy bodies. Vascular cognitive impairment. Other causes of dementia.

EXPANDING KNOWLEDGE OF DEMENTIA: Mild cognitive impairment. Staying mentally sharp. Research trends.

ACTION GUIDE FOR CAREGIVERS: Making a care plan. Being good to yourself. Activities of daily living. Good communication. Challenging behaviors. Living arrangements. Travel and safety. Health concerns.

---

113 Petersen, Ronald. ed., *Mayo Clinic Guide to Alzheimer's Disease*, 69.

Your Name Is Hughes Hannibal Shanks

I gained an entire new understanding of Alzheimer's when I read the above titled book by Lela Knox Shanks.[114] In the second stage of Alzheimer's, one of the procedures Lela Knox Shanks adopted was to make a twenty-minute audio tape of Hughes' life and let him listen to it at the beginning of the day. She gives an abbreviated version of the tape which begins "Your name is Hughes Hannibal Shanks" and then gives his address and phone number. The remainder of the tape is a catalogue of his life and achievements. What she includes and how she uses the material is most instructive for caregivers who want to be most helpful in the second stage of this disease.

The subtitle is *A Caregiver's Guide to Alzheimer's* but it is much more. I not only learned much about the daily challenges of the disease but also something of what it must feel like to be a caregiver. As a wife, she kept her husband at home and she provides some amazing things she did to accommodate his increasing disabilities. This book is my second recommendation for all seniors as a basic guide for an in-depth understanding of this disease and the nuts and bolts of what care giving involves. One of the most moving lines in the book is one I have heard from others: "I watched as he turned into someone I did not know."[115]

Some of the information Lela Knox Shanks includes in her book:

> The three stages of Alzheimer's and suggestions for
> what to do: Denial stage, Aggression and hostility,
> Brain can't tell the body what to do.

> Techniques for successful in-home management.

> The patient and cleanliness

---

114 Shanks, Lela Knox. *Your Name is Hughes Hannibal Shanks* (Lincoln, NE: University of Nebraska Press, 1996).
115 Ibid, 14.

Importance of establishing procedures.

Manual for family and caregivers.

Surviving the stress of care giving.

Coping strategies.

Help and professional services.

Outline for primary care giving training course.

Two Books and a Movie

I saw the movie *Iris* before I read either of the two books I will mention. Iris Murdoch (1919-1999) was a prolific, widely acclaimed writer (a total of thirty-three published works). She was diagnosed with Alzheimer's disease in 1997 and died two years later after being cared for almost all of that time by her husband, John Bailey. The movie is difficult to watch as a truly brilliant writer has to be told that she has indeed written novels. The end of the movie is especially heart breaking as she is pictured in a full-care facility totally in her own private world.

John Bailey, a novelist and literary critic, managed her care through all except the last few weeks. His book *Iris and the Friends: A Year of Memories*[116] describes that journey. The jacket describes it as "at times unbearably moving." In 1999, John Bailey published another book titled *Elegy for Iris.*[117] The jacket describes it in this way: "*Elegy for Iris* is a remarkable memoir of our time, an ironically joyous story about the ephemeral beauty of youth and the sobering reality of what it means to grow old." Both are reads that enlighten and disturb.

---

116 Bailey, John. *Iris and the Friends* (London: Duckworth, 1999).
117 Bailey, John. *Elegy for Iris* (New York: St. Martin's Press, 1999).

QUESTIONS FOR REFLECTION, DISCOVERY, AND CONVERSATION

1. How many of your friends and acquaintances have suffered from Alzheimer's disease? What has been your reaction/response and others in the circle of friendship and family?
2. What have been your sources of information on Alzheimer's? Which of these has been most helpful?
3. Have you seen the movie "*Iris*" or read the books by her husband? In what ways did these resources speak to you?

C
H
A
P
T
E
R
11

Do Your Interior Work and Monitor the Conversation That Never Stops

> *Therefore we do not lose heart. Though outwardly we are wasting away, yet inwardly we are being renewed day by day. (2 Corinthians 4:16).*

All of us engage in dialogues with other people through the day, but our most active and consistent is the conversation we have with ourselves.[118]

The rest of your life is going to be a continuing education, whether you sign up for it or not.[119]

---

118 McGraw, Phillip C. *Life Strategies,* 69.
119 Alda, Alan. *Things I Overheard While Talking to Myself* (New York: Random House Trade Paperbacks, 2008), 205.

It's Really the Only Way Not to Lose Heart

The words of Paul, written centuries ago, are as current as the latest self-help book. The idea that the interior life, our attitudes, our perspectives, our thoughts, etc. determine the kind of life we have *at any age,* is not, contrary to the bestseller of a few years ago, a secret. Contrary to *The Secret* (what you send out is what you get back), the teaching I would share is "what you are on the inside is finally what determines the texture and quality of your life."

Aging carries with it the inevitable losses and limitations that Paul characterize as *wasting away.* (A personal testimony: it really does feel - and look – that way!) When the nurse in an annual review asks, "Do you have difficulty with buttons?", my arthritic answer is "yes." Everything is a little harder and a little more time consuming at eighty-four than it was even at seventy-four. It takes longer to "get going" in the morning. Giving up doing my own yard work was a concession to this diminishment.

There is much that can be done in the way of regular exercise, proper vitamins and minerals, a healthier diet, etc. but the wasting away continues –outwardly. Paul admonishes that we never lose sight of the one thing that can and should increase in depth and vitality as we age – our interior lives. "There are times when I would like to shout out to the world, *The invisible part of me is not old!*"[120]

I believe that is the major reason so many seniors have told me, "I don't feel old!" Of course we don't because a major part of us is not old. Many of the suggestions in this book have to do with things to be done exteriorly that can assist us in successful aging. However, it is this invisible part of ourselves that should be a major focus *all* of our lives and especially in the later years.

We Ought to be into Spiritual Fitness

I go on record as saying that I certainly favor anything we can to do to keep the exterior of our lives in good shape. But what I fear is that far too many believe fitness is confined to the realm of

120 Seymour, Robert E. *Aging Without Apology,* 4.

the physical. Yes, we ought to be into physical fitness but we must likewise be into spiritual fitness. Spiritual fitness for me has to do with everything we are as persons – our total beings. As physical strength wanes, spiritually we ought to grow stronger. As we shrink in stature, spiritually we ought to become giants.

"The second half of life presents us with the opportunity to develop increased depth, integrity, and character – or not."[121] Cultivating the interior life means many things but surely for most of us in the faith community it includes what Paul calls the fruit of the Spirit: *love, joy, peace, patience, kindness, generosity, faithfulness, gentleness, and self-control* (Galatians 5:22).

In a conference at Furman University, I remember hearing John Powell tell of one of his experiences as a seminarian. He went to the infirmary one night and observed one of the brothers tucking in two bedridden priests. The same thing was done in each room; the blanket was tucked up under the chin. When it was done to the first man he looked up and said, "Get your face out of mine! What do you think this is?" When the same thing was done for the second man, he said, "Oh, brother, you are so good to us. Thank you. And before I fall asleep tonight I'll say a special prayer for you. Thank you, brother." John Powell said that as he stood there and witnessed both scenes he thought to himself: "Someday I will be one of those two old men. Which one? I don't make the decision in old age. I'm making it right now."

VOICES WITHOUT AND WITHIN

"Modern man (sic) is bombarded with so many voices that he no longer hears any. Least of all his own."[122] So many voices are vying for our attention (and they keep turning up the volume) that we find it almost impossible to listen to any singular one with full attention. How many things can you listen to at once? Is it possible to multi-listen? There is no doubt that:

121 Arrien, Angeles. *The Second Half of Life*, 5.
122 Wiesel, Elie. *From the Kingdom of Memory* (New York: Schocken Books, 1990), 41.

We all hear voices....At least I do. Some of them are distorted and destructive; they speak to me thoughts of envy and resentment and fear. Some of them are healthy and strong; they speak words of love and truth. The ones I listen to shape my life.[123]

As a "primary" in Sunday school, I remember the song that contained the line: "Be careful little ears what you hear." In spite of the often negative connotation of the phrase, I advocate "selective hearing." Because the voices we listen to shape our lives, we need to be very selective in those we allow to make their way into the interior of our beings. In our present culture, there are far too many voices of anger and fear that characterize the "dialogue" carried on in the political and social arenas.

The *Mayo Clinic on Healthy Aging* advises: "Watch your attitude. You are what you think."[124]   And you can't help thinking about what you are listening to. Whenever a strong emotion seems to overpower us, we need to ask, "What are the thoughts that have contributed to this feeling?" and "Where did this attitude come from?"

Jordan B. Peterson in *12 Rules for Life* gives much we need to ponder:

> The people I listen to need to talk, because that's how people think.
>
> Thinking is listening to yourself. It's difficult. To think, you have to be at least two people at the same time. Then you have to let those people disagree. Thinking is an internal dialogue between two or more different views of the world.
>
> True thinking is complex and demanding. It requires you to be articulate speaker and careful, judicious listener, at the same time. It involves conflict. Conflict involves negotiation and compromise. So, you have to learn to give and take and

---

123 Ortberg, John. *God is Closer Than You Think* (Grand Rapids: Zondervan, (2005), 79.
124 Creagan, Edward T. ed., *Mayo Clinic on Healthy Aging*, 14.

to modify your premises and adjust your thoughts – even your perceptions of the world. [125]

THREE IMPORTANT TRUTHS ABOUT THIS INNER CONVERSATION

1. You can't shut it off. "There's always a conversation in your head about your environment, the people around you, and, most important, about yourself. You can't shut it off."[126] Rather than attempting to shut it off, my advice is to do some intensive listening. This means you have to find a time and a place to shut out the noise and conversations that are going on around you. Here we are back at the need for silence and quiet in your life. I have never wondered why we are told that Jesus spent large units of his time alone and in prayer – frequently all night. For me, that is one of the largest ingredients in his ability to say the things he said and do the things he did.

2. This good listening calls for self-reflection. "Effective emotional knowledge demands a profound level of self-reflection..."[127] Many of these inner conversations are loaded with emotions and self-reflection is necessary in order to elevate the EQ we talked about earlier. We don't suddenly conclude, "I know why I had that reaction. I know why I said what I did. I know why I felt the way I did." These revelations don't come without honest self-reflection.

3. "My inner monologue simply can't be trusted. It has to be held up and cross-examined in the light of the truth."[128] With truth in such short supply in the current culture, this might seem like an impossible challenge. We begin our search for truth with giving our best efforts to being

---

125 Peterson, Jordan B. *12 Rules for Life*, 240-242.
126 Greitens, Eric. *Resilience*, 176.
127 Kreamer, Anne. *It's Always Something*, 15.
128 Hansen, Brant. *Blessed Are the Misfits* (Nashville: W Publishing, 2017), 158.

honest with ourselves – not giving ourselves a pass by attributing our words or behavior to pure motives (all motives are mixed). This is one reason many people have a spiritual advisor with whom they can check out their interpretation of their inner monologue. Some friendships are deep and trusting enough that you can use that friend as a sounding-board. "Am I seeing this correctly? Is my interpretation valid? Do I bring too much prejudice to the table to be able to see this for what it is?" These are just examples of questions that can open the door to helpful conversation about the inner dialogue.

Dag Hammerskjold once noted: "The more you listen to the voice within you, the better you will hear what is sound outside."[129] I believe there are several reasons for this. The first is, the more we learn to listen to the voice within, the more we learn how to listen to the voices of others. Listening is a discipline, a discipline that takes concentration and practice. It has to begin with "non-judgmental listening." That applies both to ourselves and to others. Prejudicial listening is not really listening to others; it is turning up our own voice that prevents our hearing precisely what the other person is saying. If we don't do this kind of listening to our own voices I don't believe we will be able to do it for others.

Once we begin to understand how complex and often conflicted we are it brings a greater degree of genuine empathy as we listen to others. I remember reading about the Pastor's class for children in which the question was asked, "If all the good people in the world were green and all the bad people in the world were purple, what color would you be?" One little girl immediately spoke up, "I'd be streaky!" Once we discover and admit the streakiness within, it opens the door to better and clearer conversation with others.

The need for patience with ourselves comes right on the heels of the above comments. To live as imperfect human beings in an imperfect world sets the stage for confession, redemption, and

---

129 Buford, Bob. *Half Time*, 112.

patience as we continue our journey. You may not be familiar with Brennan Manning but I encourage you to become acquainted with him. He is refreshing and challenging but most of all he is affirming of all of us in this human predicament. Manning writes: "Some people might say the line 'God loves you as you are, not as you should be' is synonymous with the name Brennan Manning. I would say they're right...."[130]

To listen to ourselves in this context is to enable us to hear things we would never be able to hear and to bring things out of their secret hiding places. When we listen to others in this same context - God loves them as they are, not as they should be- we begin to listen on an entirely new level. Just try it. Of course, first, with yourself.

QUESTIONS FOR REFLECTION, DISCOVERY, AND CONVERSATION

1. As you have aged, in what ways have you attempted not to lose heart?
2. How are you maintaining your spiritual fitness?
3. In what ways do you regulate, monitor, and evaluate your inner conversation? Which of the suggestions in his chapter did you find most helpful?

---

130 Manning, Brennan. *All Is Grace* (Colorado Springs: David C. Cook, (2011), 107.

C
H
A
P
T
E
R

12

Continue to Develop the Unique Person You Are

Setting the Stage

> The novelist May Sarton at age 70 realized, "I am more myself than ever before.[131]

> "We teach not so much by what we know as by what we are." J. G. Fitch.[132]

> While performing his daily routine of cello practice, the 91-year-old Pablo Casals was once asked by one of his students, "Master, why do you continue to practice?" Casals answered, "Because I am making progress."[133]

The Uniqueness That Belongs to Each of Us

This is not meant to be an endorsement of the oft heard disclaimer, "Well, that's just the way I am." I often want to reply (but never do), "Well, is that the way you think you are supposed to be?" The uniqueness that belongs to us is has nothing to do with

---

131 Valliant, George E. *Aging Well*, 141.
132 Schofield, Stephen. ed., *In Search of C. S. Lewis*, 47.
133 Valliant, George E. *Aging Well*, 214.

irresponsible behavior or the self-centeredness of some in every generation who can be labeled the "me generation." The uniqueness that belongs to each of us is represented by the phrases, "I was at my best today" and "He isn't himself today." It is summarized as being the person God has created us to be. And this person is *always* a person in relationship. This person is *always* a person who knows the truth of Acts 20:35: *It is more blessed to give than to receive.*

"You will do better in work, life, and relationships when you are acting in accord with who you truly are, versus trying to be someone you are not."[134] I remember hearing John Powell say in a workshop, "If I'm not going to be myself, who am I going to be?" One of my recent reads is about the life and work of Fred Rogers, *The Good Neighbor* by Maxwell King. Roger's son, John, was interviewed by a *New York Times* reporter and asked how it felt to be Fred Roger's son. His reply:

> "Well, it's hard to make a comparison, because he's the only father I have." He added, "I thought, I hope you don't think that's smart-alecky....Dad's very normal and natural. He's not a Clint Eastwood or some high-powered actor. He's himself. He's himself, and he wants us to be ourselves, and... to be comfortable. He's not a fancy person."[135]

What struck me as I read the book was just how "down to earth" Rogers was. He disarmed his critics by being the person with them he was in *Mr. Roger's Neighborhood.* That is who he was – at all times. Not a single person ever contradicted this assessment of the famous television personality.

I would say, he was real. He did not have a television personality, a public personality, and an at-home personality. He was authentic. Authenticity is a mark of the uniqueness that belongs to him. An underscored line in one of my books is: "In order to give your life to others, you must first have a life to give."[136]

---

134 Cloud, Henry. *Never Go Back* (New York: Howard Books, 2014), 37.
135 King, Maxwell. *The Good Neighbor,* 302.
136 Cloud, Henry. *Never Go Back,* 38.

Discovering and Implementing That Uniqueness is the Work of a Lifetime

I believe this discovery begins by finding what you love to do, what your passion is, what you believe your calling to be and letting that become your priority. An eighty-six-year-old man in ICU told Mildred Tengbom:

> "God has given the wife and me sixty wonderful years together," he said, gasping as he spoke, "and as if that wasn't enough, he let me do work I loved."
> "What work gave you so much satisfaction and joy?" I asked.
> "Paperhanging," he said.[137]

He then explained why this had been so. It's quite a read but I summarize it by saying: he was truly blessed. Too many believe in this culture with its peculiar definition of success, you must make a real splash in order to be counted as anybody of significance. My philosophy is that the first requirement in achievement is to be significant to yourself. My prime example: "Brother Lawrence called himself 'the lord of all pots and pans' because he never got higher on the organizational chart than cook and bottle-washer."[138]

I've never seen a bumper sticker that read, "My son is a dishwasher at the University." How would you live down that shame! It is such a shame that is such a shame! We can bring dignity to any work we do. "What will the neighbors think?" is not a question worthy of asking but it seems to be the unspoken question in back of far too many decisions we make. To be a paperhanger or a dishwasher or a trash collector or a street cleaner is to perform a necessary function and fill an essential role.

---

137 Tengbom, Mildred. *Moving Into a New Now* (Minneapolis: Augsburg, 1997), 70.
138 Ortberg, John. *God is Closer Than You Think*, 59.

"Ignatius's most fundamental teaching was that individuals had to find the way that suited them best."[139] It seems to me that every New Testament verse that speaks about accountability day (usually called Judgment Day) has the basic criterion of faithfulness. Faithfulness to the gifts that are yours. Faithfulness to the calling you have received. Brother Lawrence washed pots and pans for the glory of God. Wonder what kind of a change would come in our lives if we were able to view the necessary, mundane, and often menial tasks of life as opportunities to offer gifts for the glory of God? This may be just another way of finding the sacred in the ordinary.

How Did We Move From Character to Personality?

As the twentieth century dawned, Warren Susman observed in his work Culture as History, the great change that was under way. The words that had peppered the advice manuals of an earlier generation, words, that came out of a moral world, were disappearing. These were words like "duty," "golden deeds," "morals," "manners," "honor," "citizenship," and "reputation." But as the new century began, a different set of interests came into view. These were signaled by the prominence in the advice manuals of words like "fascinating," "stunning," "attractive," "glowing," "masterful," "creative," "dominant," "forceful." The words most common earlier had been the words of character: these new words were those of personality.... Character is good or bad: personality is attractive, forceful, or magnetic.[140]

Those words from older advice manuals need to be revived in our time. Those words were the building blocks of what has been termed "the greatest generation." Their contributions and sacrifices came not from the desire to be celebrities but from the commitment to make a lasting contribution to their world. Their

---

139 Martin, James. *The Jesuit Guide to Almost Everything* (New York: HarperOne, 2010), 20.
140 Wells, David F. *The Courage To Be Protestant*, 147.

watchwords were duty and honor. The focus was on something much larger than themselves which seems rather strange to mention in a chapter dealing with the need to continue to develop the unique person you were created to be. The emphasis on personality keeps our attention on how we look to others, how we are coming across, what impression we are making. The emphasis on character keeps our attention on the kind of persons we are at the very core of our beings. It is following Jesus' admonition to make certain that the tree is good and healthy as the way to ensure that the fruit will be first quality. *By their fruit you will recognize them.... Every good tree bears good fruit, but a bad tree bears bad fruit* (Matthew 7:16-17).

> ## "WE CANNOT KNOW WHICH OF THE POSSIBLE FUTURES WILL HAPPEN, BUT WE CAN KNOW THAT WE WILL ENTER THE FUTURE TAKING OURSELVES WITH US."[141]

The one certainty about my future is that I will be in it. You cannot predict that future, but you can determine the kind of person you want to be in that future.

> A memorial tribute for a nun who died at the age of ninety-nine included these words from a superior's letter to her: "There are so many things for which my head and my heart say 'Thank you' to you that I can't even list them. But I believe most of all I am thankful to God that always, through the long years, I find you always you."[142]

Maintaining the integrity of who we are and continuing to work on being the person we believe God has called us to be, is the best way I know to provide stability for ourselves and for those around us. Did you ever work with someone you were never sure just who they were going to be when you met them in the morning? You were never sure which personality they were donning for

141 Broyles, Stephen E. *The Wind That Destroys and Heals* (Colorado Springs: Shaw Books, 2003).
142 Fischer, Kathleen. *Imaging Life After Death*, 16.

the day. The words spoken about the nun in the above quote is the same tribute given by so many in our earlier references to Fred Rogers.

"If there is only one insight you take away from this book, though, I hope it's a newfound sense of entitlement to be yourself. I can vouch personally for the life-transforming effects of this outlook."[143] After that first sentence, in the book I added "your best self." The sub-title of Cain's book is *The Power of Introverts in a World That Can't Stop Talking.* In this section I feel it is necessary to add something I too often assume people take for granted. We are always working on becoming our best selves. We are works in progress. We are always under construction. Molly Howard, as a teacher at Jefferson County High School in Louisville, Georgia, developed a new system of grading. She gave grades of A, B, C, and NY. The NY stands for Not Yet. "There's no 'never' at Jefferson anymore, only a 'Not Yet.'"[144]

When anyone asks me if I am the best version of myself, my answer is, "I'm still getting a grade of NY, Not Yet." But that does not mean I am unable to continue to be the unique person I was created to be. There is no perfection in any of the dimensions of our humanity, only a continual becoming. But that continual becoming needs always to be consistent with the uniqueness that belongs to each of us.

---

143 Cain, Susan. *Quiet,* 15.
144 Health, Chip & Dan Heath. *Switch* (New York: Broadman Books, 2010), 173-174.

QUESTIONS FOR REFLECTION, DISCOVERY, AND CONVERSATION

1. Have you found that discovering and developing the uniqueness that belongs to you is the work of a lifetime? How are you working on it?
2. How do you think the culture moved from character to personality? What have been the effects of this shift?
3. How does Pablo Casals underscore the validity of using the NY grade as an encouragement for lifelong development?

CHAPTER 13

BE PROACTIVE AND CLAIM RESPONSIBILITY FOR YOUR OWN LIFE

SETTING THE STAGE

I asked the sister in charge, "Why are they like that? Why can't you see a smile on their faces?"[145]

The sister answered, "The same thing always happens. They are always waiting for someone to come and visit them...They do not stop looking. Nobody comes."[146]

The three words our culture has in the wrong order: Feelings, Action, Identity....If you want to feel differently, act differently.[123]

Bottom line: You are accountable for the life you have, and how you feel and react to it.[147]

---

145 Mother Teresa. *In the Heart of the World* (Novato, CA: New World Library, 1999), 65-66.

146 Greitens, Eric. *Resilience,* 79, 81.

147 McGraw, Philip C. *Life Strategies,* 81.

The Problem With "Waiting for Your Ship to Come In."

When I was growing up I heard on many occasions the phrase, "I'm waiting for my ship to come in." It indicated a hope that something good would come sailing into their lives. They were waiting for something good to happen. They were waiting for good luck to find them. They were living in the passive rather than the active mode. They were like the people in the nursing home waiting for someone to come and visit them rather than picking up the telephone and making a connection themselves or dropping a note to those they would like to see. (This applies only to those who were physically and mentally able to do this.)

We soon discover early in life that being proactive makes the possibility of good things coming our way much more likely. One of Thomas Edison's most famous quotes is: "Opportunity is missed by most people because it is dressed in overalls and looks like work."[148] My mother and dad both believed in hard work when that was necessary just to provide the necessities of life for a family of six. Because they were able-bodied, they were not sitting at home waiting for handouts. They felt it was their responsibility to provide for themselves and their family. They assumed responsibility for themselves as they had done all of their lives.

The basic question, "Who is responsible for my life?" has one basic answer, "I am." My wife's mother frequently underscored this principle by echoing her favorite saying: "Every tub sets on its own bottom." The Scriptures render the same verdict: *"So then, we will all give an account of ourselves to God"* (Romans 14:12). This is not a threat, it is simply a fact. If I'm not responsible for myself, who is? "The devil made me do it," is the classic evasion going back to the Garden of Eden. The late Flip Wilson had a classic routine in which he assumed the role of Geraldine, a minister's wife. She had been warned not to buy any more dresses and, of course, returns home from shopping with a dress. When asked why she bought

---

148 Peck, M. Scott. *An Anthology of Wisdom*, 168.

it, her story goes through several stages of temptation from the devil until, after trying it on in the store, she pleads that she had no choice. "He pulled a gun on me!" The absurdity of all of our excuses becomes as plain as day as we get a good laugh at ourselves.

Although we become more limited in our choices and options as we age, as long we remain competent, we remain responsible for ourselves. This keeps us proactive and saves us from the blame game and membership in the poor me club. We can't wait until we are old to take this stance. Although it is true that as we get older we become more and more of what we already are, it is never too late to stop the waiting and hoping and, under the circumstances in which we find ourselves, assume whatever control of our lives it is possible to exercise.

Do It! Do It! Do It!

That is the title of a book I gave my younger son years ago. Its ~~It's~~ obvious call to action remains a central ingredient for successful aging. Jonathan Morris in *The Way to Serenity* has a chapter titled "In God's Eyes We Are All Action Figures." He discusses Jesus' parable of the sheep and the goats (Matthew 25:31-40), closing with this comment: "He doesn't mention a single thing they (the goats) have done wrong! Their crime was inaction, not their action."[149] Most of the time we do not need to be asking ourselves "How do I feel about this?" but, rather, "What am I going to *do* about this?" Whether it is a decision to be made or a step to be taken, there is usually always something to be done on our part that puts us back into the management role of some aspect of our lives.

A twist on the quote at the beginning of this chapter is: "We don't feel our way into new actions, we act our way into new feelings." Some of Jesus' commandments about loving our enemies, going the second mile, turning the other cheek, and doing good to those who have done harm to us sound ridiculous because we know we would not *feel* like doing these things. Doing what you

149 Morris, Jonathan. *The Way to Serenity* (New York: HarperCollins, 2014), 123.

know is right, regardless of how you feel, is not being hypocritical. I certainly did not feel like getting up at two o'clock in the morning to get a bottle of milk for the baby. I did it because it was the right thing to do and it was my responsibility. Neither of my sons later told me how hypocritical I was for not being overjoyed at the opportunity to feed them. They simply enjoyed the bottle of milk.

Richard Rohr is one of my highly recommended authors. One of his words of wisdom that may at first seem highly unorthodox is: "Jesus clearly taught orthopraxy (right behavior) much more than orthodoxy (right ideas or right beliefs).[150] For me, this is why the Sermon on the Mount ends with a crash instead of an amen. The person who builds a house on sand is like the person who listens to Jesus' teaching and does not put it into practice. Does not take action on it.

As we get older, it is more important than ever to put into action the things we know will improve life for us and those around us. From Eric Greitens' book *Resilience:* "Today I'm writing about the single most important habit to build if you want to be resilient: the habit of taking responsibility for your life."[151] How do you bounce back when something has knocked you off your feet? How do you get life started in a new direction? How do you begin to repair damaged relationships? How do you keep resilience in your life? Greitens is correct: by taking responsibility for your life. Whether you call it "taking the bull by the horns" or some less combative metaphor, it all boils down to the simple decision, "I'm going to *do* something about this."

John Wesley Had It Right

Most know this advice from John Wesley: "Do all the good you can, By all the means you can, In all the ways you can, In all the places you can, At all the times you can, To all the people you can, As long as ever you can."[152] This is the best prescription for

---

150 Rohr, Richard with Jon Bookser Feister. *Hope Against Darkness,* 160.
151 Greitens, Eric. *Resilience,* 101.
152 Peck, M. Scott. *An Anthology of Wisdom,* 264.

happiness for us older folk than anything else I have ever read. It describes a life of action, purpose, resolve, and an outward focus that keeps us from forever being obsessed with our aches, pains, and misfortunes.

Maintain Connections

> Eric Pfeiffer from a long-term study on older Americans found that people who age successfully "stay in training" throughout their adult life in three major areas: physical activity, psychological and intellectual activity, and social relationships.[153]

The number one complaint I received through the years from people in nursing homes was what has been termed the modern plague: loneliness.[154] This is the plague of being disconnected and it becomes extreme in places like assisted-care facilities. In my visitation, the last word any resident said to me was, "Come back to see me...soon!" The need to maintain connections before this kind of seclusion occurs cannot be overemphasized. We are made for community, for social relationships. The cultivation of these relationships takes time, effort, and face-to-face encounters. I've never had a person in a nursing home request, "Please text me whenever you can." The only request is: "Come to *see* me."

One complaint about those of us in our later years is that we keep telling our stories – and sometimes we repeat them! Of course! Listening to each other's stories is the way we come to know each other, to understand each other, to feel connected to one another. As a part of all my intentional interims, I did a series of workshops that included discussion sessions at tables of eight. The questions were supplied and then for twenty to thirty minutes people just talked to one another. After six months, a number of people would come to me and say, "I thought I knew the members of this congregation but now I realize I never really knew them until I heard

---

153 Chopra, Deepak. *Ageless Body, Timeless Mind*, 82.
154 Wells, David F. *The Courage To Be Protestant*, 33.

their stories." A major purpose of the interim was to provide a safe setting for people to have genuine conversations with one another that went beyond the brief exchange of greetings before a Sunday worship service.

"People who are happy, passionate about their work, and engaged daily with friends and family live a lot longer than people who are depressed and isolated."[155] Even though our formal "work" is ended, regardless of age, we can still find work that belongs to us. In one of my churches, a homebound arthritic senior, spent each morning clipping articles from the newspaper that highlighted an accomplishment of some sort. She sent a personal note (most often to people she had never met) congratulating them on their achievement. Whenever I visited her, she would regale me with the many calls and letters she had received in response to her notes. She was as happy as any senior I have ever known. Plus: her family and friends visited her frequently because she was such a delight to be around.

"One day when I was holding my three-year-old daughter Annie, I spontaneously asked her, 'How come you are so nice?' She clasped her hands around my neck and answered immediately – Because you love me.'"[156] I believe the power Jesus used to change people was to love them. Biblically, love redeems, transforms, reshapes, renews, and enables a person to love because of the love that has been received. Maintaining connections means maintaining those relationships of love that will enable us to feel love and allow that love to keep our lives in the positive mode. A smile, the touch of a hand, a sentimental card, the simple words "I love you," not only transform our day, they transform us. And that enables us to be in the transforming business ourselves.

You might want to skip to the Addendum and read "The Necessity of On-Going Forgiveness" which plays an indispensible role in maintaining those connections.

---

155 Mitteldorf, Josh & Dorion Sagan. *Cracking the Code,* 225.
156 Rohr, Richard. *Grace in Action* (New York: Crossroad Publishing Company, 1994), 41.

QUESTIONS FOR REFLECTION, DISCOVERY, AND CONVERSATION

1. What is the basic problem of waiting for someone to visit you in the nursing home or waiting for your ship to come in?
2. Why does action come before feeling? Do you believe that in the Sermon on the Mount Jesus taught orthopraxy?
3. Do you believe most seniors are proactive in maintaining connections? How have you attempted to do this?

CHAPTER 14

TAP THE RESOURCES OF FAITH AND HOPE

SETTING THE STAGE

Robert Ellsberg speaking of Dorothy Day: "She read the news in the light of eternity.[157]

Every molecule of iron in your bloodstream originated in the fusion of elements in the heart of a star.[158]

We are not human beings trying to become spiritual. That task has already been done for us by our initial creation as "images of God" (Genesis 1:26). We are already spiritual beings. That is God's gift. Our desperate and needed task, the one we have not succeeded at very well after all these centuries, is how to become human....Most of the world is so tired of "spiritual people." We would be happy just to meet some real human beings....[159]

157 Wicks, Robert. *No Problem* (Notre Dame: Sorin Books, 2014), 9.
158 Taylor, John V. *The Easter God* (New York: Continuum, 2003), 77.
159 Rohr, Richard. *Soul Brothers* (Maryknoll, NY: Orbis Books, 2004), 119-120.

THE BATTLE BETWEEN SCIENCE AND RELIGION

I've lost count of the books on my shelves that deal in some way with what is termed the ongoing battle between science and religion. Although out of the date, the following quote gives the essence of that battle:

> In some universities it is actually fashionable to teach that what cannot be measured does not exist. The arrogance of it is extraordinary. We presume that our little rules and clocks can encompass Reality. Rather than recognize our limitations, we strive to limit the world. Unable to cut it down to our size, we deny the immeasurable.[160]

I stand with those who maintain that there is no battle between true science and true religion. Science deals with the physical universe and what can be counted, weighed, measured, and tested. It deals with how things work. Religion deals with the why of existence and the exploration of another reality other than the one that is measurable. It seeks to answer the question posed by Peggy Lee's famous song, "Is that all there is?" It seeks to explore Jack Nicholson's quandary in a movie as he walks through the waiting room of a psychiatrist's office: "What if this is as good as it gets?" We are constantly searching and seeking and longing for something more and beyond.

Sociologist Peter Berger wrote: "If anything characterizes modernity, it is the loss of the sense of transcendence – a reality that exceeds and encompasses our everyday affairs."[161] It is difficult for me to understand how people can have such reservations in light of the discoveries we have made about the depth, extent, and mysteries of the universe – both telescopic and microscopic. No one in the recent past ever envisioned the complexity of matter that we now know to exist. We thought we could measure and test everything

---

160 Peck, M. Scott, with Marilyn Von Waldner, *Gifts for the Journey* (New York: HarperSanFrancisco, 1995), 110.
161 Ortberg, John. *Who Is This Man?* (Grand Rapids: Zondervan, 2012), 151.

in the physical world. Now we know we can't. So much is beyond measurement, testing, and explanation.

INFINITY AND BEYOND

Photographs from the Hubble telescope revealed that what had previously been seen as unfocused blobs of light were galaxies, which scientists now believe may number at least 10,000 million, each with at least 100,000 million stars.[162] The author of that information guesses that comes out to about 1,600 galaxies for every person on earth. When church dignitaries refused to look through Galileo's telescope because they already knew what was there, even Galileo could not begin to imagine what was there.

As long as you let the Bible speak to what it speaks to and let science speak to what it is able to speak to, you are on safe ground. The Bible begins with the faith statement, *In the beginning, God created the heavens and the earth.* It does not go into details of the how or the scope of that creation. The speaking of the world into existence in six "days" has nothing to do with twenty-four hour days resulting in the thesis that the world was created in 4004 B.C. (a marginal note you will find in the Scofield Bible). The Bible speaks to the Who of creation. That is beyond the scope of science – meaning: science cannot prove that isn't true.

The Creation Museum located in the northern part of my state of Kentucky, has done a great disservice to the cause of religion and faith in our time. In the vestibule of the main building, there is a small dinosaur wearing a saddle. The tour guide (I am told, I haven't been) explains that dinosaurs and human beings were on the earth at the same time. The smaller dinosaurs were tamed and ridden like horses. A part of the other disinformation is that the fossils in the earth were laid down during the great biblical flood which also carved out the Grand Canyon. (My geology course in a Christian college taught me that such theories are disproved by science.) Too many moderns believe that those of us in the faith

162 Mayne, Michael. *Learning to Dance* (London: Darton, Longman and Todd, 2001), 47-48.

community hold these kinds of beliefs. Again, I have no problem with true science and true faith (religion).

> Only five percent of the universe, bodies, planets, stars, nebulae, galaxies, is sensible matter; the rest is "dark matter" and the more elusive "dark energy" – Einstein's "cosmic constant" true, so it turns out, filling the void with itself in its own image, present everywhere, visible nowhere, establishing itself out of the known and unknown. Invisibility. Omnipresence. God?[163]

If that quote doesn't leave you scratching your head, you need to go back and read it again! Ecclesiastes 3:11: *He (God) has made everything beautiful in its time. He has also set eternity in the human heart; yet no one can fathom what God has done from beginning to end.* Some have called this the view from eternity. This is not unlike Dorothy Day's reading the news in the light of eternity. There is within us that pull, that sense of a much wider, deeper, and timelessness that is not earthbound.

When the Psalmist wrote, *I praise you because I am fearfully and wonderfully made* (Psalm 139:14), he had no idea just how fearful and wonderful that is. "Within our bodies are something like 50 trillion different cells, all inter-relating to keep us alive and healthy....Each cell in my body carries the instruction book for 100,00 genes."[164] When I think that I was once part of a star (see quote at beginning of chapter) and begin to realize the unbelievable complexity (and ingenuity!) of the human body, I almost have to rethink what is meant by the term "mere mortal." This kind of information gives new weight and meaning to the biblical teaching that we are created in the image of God.

---

163 Domina, Lynn, ed., *Poets on the Psalms* (San Antonia: Trinity University Press, 2008), 172.
164 Mayne, Michael. *Learning to Dance,* 98-99.

We Can't Avoid the Word 'Mystery'

> Physics has discovered that when you get to the smallest
> point (atomic particles) and the biggest point (galaxies and
> black hole) – it's mystery again! It looks knowable, yet finally
> it's unknowable when you reach the edges. Control eventually
> gives way to mystery and the letting go of control.[165]

When I talk about tapping the resources of faith and hope, I'm
talking about resources that go beyond the knowable, the measurable, the controllable – the things we have been encountering all of
our lives, not just in old age. Adam and Eve were convinced (with
a little outside help) that once they ate of the Tree of Knowledge
they would be their own gods and nothing would be beyond their
understanding and control. Many continue to live under that same
illusion. My by-line in almost every workshop is: If mystery, para-
dox, and ambiguity are not part of your life and faith you're going
to have real difficulties making any sense of existence.

In old age we are brought face to face with the fact that we
need outside help in areas we once managed without difficulty. To
live by faith and hope is to acknowledge that this outside help is not
limited to any age or only to crisis moments. "One study found
that blood pressure of older adults who attended religious services
at least once a week and prayed or studied the Bible daily was
consistently lower than those who did not."[166] I'm so glad I found
that in the *Mayo Clinic on Healthy Aging;* it is a well researched and
documented piece of information. Of course these activities help.
We are spiritual beings and we are simply getting in touch with an
essential part of our beings.

---

165 Rohr, Richard, with Jon Bookser Feister, *Hope Against Darkness,* 11.
166 Creagan, Edward T. ed., *Mayo Clinic on Healthy Aging,* 77.

QUESTIONS FOR REFLECTION, DISCOVERY, AND CONVERSATION

1. What was most helpful for you in this chapter? What was most challenging?
2. How do you go about reading the news in the light of eternity?
3. How does acknowledging mystery still allow us to live by faith/trust?

15

LEARN TO NEGOTIATE WELL THE ENDINGS AND BEGINNINGS THAT ARE A PART OF ALL LIFE

SETTING THE STAGE

> *Every hello that has ever been spoken has had a goodbye tucked away somewhere deep inside, waiting for some moving day or some graduation day or some retiring or relocating or dying day, some eventual, inevitable someday when the goodbye that was hidden in the hello will find its way out into the open.*[167]

> *Carl Jung: "We cannot live the afternoon of life according to the program of life's morning."*[168]

> *Someone has quipped that the three great temptations of old age are: to whine, decline, or recline.... My experience has been that many older people shine with a contagious optimism and a creative spirit that becomes a role model for all generations.*

---

167 Poole, Charles E. *The Tug of Home* (Macon: Peake Road, 1997), 79.
168 Scott, Willard. *The Older the Fiddle, the Better the Tune*, 159.

Beautiful young people are accidents of nature:
beautiful older people are works of art.[169]

Tell Me It Isn't So!

The first quote above I used in one of my earlier books (*All I Need to Know I'm Still Learning At 80*) in a chapter titled "It's All About Endings and Beginnings." As much as we don't like to face it, sooner or later (it's usually later) we learn the truth of the ancient line, "This, too, will pass away...." We try a thousand different ways to "capture" the times in life which seem to overflow with joy and happiness. Those times when everything just seemed to be coming up roses now don't seem to be as frequent as we were promised they would be and we have found no way to keep those roses from fading and dying.

We don't want to believe that every hello has a goodbye tucked away somewhere deep inside (and frequently not so deep after all). A popular song of my youth had the line, "Those were the days, my friends, we thought they'd never end." I am not suggesting that we ought to become "reality checkers" in all such times by announcing, "We know that nothing lasts forever." It is only natural to feel that the good times will keep rolling, the people we love will always be around, the world as we know and love it will remain essentially the same, and time would never be so cruel as to write "finish" on what we love most. But time is "like an ever-rolling stream" and it does finally "bear away" everything as it used to be.

But those goodbyes do not signal the end of life, they signal a transition that is less difficult to make in later years if we have given attention and creative effort to earlier transitions. Endings begin very early in life and so often they go "unattended." Joan Chittister's book *The Way We Were* has a chapter titled "A Story of Conversion and Renewal." In that chapter she writes: "If truth

---

169 Ibid, 159.

were known, most people seldom really recognize when one thing has served its purpose and another needs to begin.[170]

> **"THERE ARE TWO WORDS THAT GROW MORE IMPORTANT AS ONE GETS OLDER. THEY ARE 'OVER' AND 'NEXT.'"** (Norman Lear).[171]

The word "over" usually doesn't ~~not~~ come quickly or easily. With many of our endings there must follow a period of grief. One woman lamented: "My old life is gone. How come nobody talks about that? They congratulate you on your new life, but I have to mourn the old life alone."[172] I suspect this has to do with the universal desire to stay positive in life and to get over losses as quickly as possible. Even though it is a big mistake and not emotionally healthy, it continues to persist in a culture that seeks to keep the focus on what lies ahead. But "over" does require time for mourning and fortunate are those who have friends who will not only allow them to do this but will also stand with them as they do so.

When we lost our older son in 2013, it was the biggest loss that Pat and I had ever experienced and we are still working on structuring our lives without Mark. It is a process, it is difficult, it takes time, and it involves continuing to grieve that goodbye. We have definitely made progress but when anyone asks, "When do you think things will get back to normal?" our reply is, "They won't. Things will never be the same again." That's what an ending is all about. Working on bringing realistic and healthy closure to this "over" is necessary if we are to be able to take healthy advantage of the word "next."

I maintain that although there is a goodbye tucked deep inside every hello, there is also another "hello" waiting to be spoken in a new beginning. And I'm also convinced that when we whisper

---

170 Chittister, Joan. *The Way We Were*, 51.
171 Scott, Willard. *The Older the Fiddle, the Better the Tune*, 103.
172 Bridges, William. *Transitions: Making Sense of Life's Changes* (Reading, MA: Addison-Wesley Publishing Company, 1980), 11.

that final "Goodbye" there is the biggest "Hello" of all waiting to be shouted!

What is important is to recognize that "over" is not the only word life has to offer. It is not the final word that life has to offer. The "next" may be impossible to recognize at the beginning of the process and then it may not be easily achieved. That's why maturity and wisdom need to be a large part of what we have achieved throughout our lives. Those are two of the assets that aging is meant to bring. That is why everything we have talked about so far in this book is so important. If throughout our lives we have been able to hear the word "over," grieve something that is to be no more, assess what that ending means in our lives, and analyze exactly what the word "next" means, we will be far better equipped to hear these two words in our later years.

For a new beginning, Hugh Prather suggests there are three things we need to let go: Judging, controlling, and being right. "Release these three and you will have the whole mind and twinkly heart of a child."[173]

"MY LIFE HAS BEEN NOTHING BUT A SERIES OF NEW BEGINNINGS" (JOAN CHITTISTER).[174]

Isn't this true for all of us? Isn't this what life is all about?

> Wayne Flynt: "According to contemporary Gallup polls, Americans rated 1957 the happiest year ever recorded. That fall, I began my senior year of high school and had I been polled I would have agreed."[175]

That was the year I was graduated from college and began my first year in the seminary. I would agree that the world seemed much less complex then and more people seemed to be less anxious, less frustrated, less confused, and happier. Why not bring back

---

173 Prather, Hugh. *The Little Book of Letting Go*, 17.

174 Chittister, Joan. *The Gift of Years*, xii.

175 Flynt, Wayne. *Keeping the Faith* (Tuscaloosa: The University of Alabama Press, 2011), 57.

1957? Why not relive that year over and over again? It may seem like a foolish question with an obvious answer but that still does not prevent many of us from attempting something similar whenever we attempt to live the present by what was true in the past.

In September 1987, the California Angels had an insurmountable lead going in the late innings. They blew the lead and lost the game. After the game, a sportswriter made his way through the silent, somber locker room to talk with one of the Angels' star players, a veteran of many seasons. The sportswriter said, "Well, I guess that must be one of the most bitter losses of your entire career," to which the player responded with quiet wisdom and unforgettable insight, "Yes. It was a difficult and disappointing loss, and it hurts, but that one is over now, and we'll just have to stop wanting that one."[176]

There would have been no better way to cripple the new season which lay ahead than to continue to bemoan the bitter loss of the last season. There was no better way to cripple 1958 than to insist on a rerun of 1957. The secret of moving forward is to view the "next" as a new beginning. Life is meant to be a series of new beginnings. It is meant to be moving ahead with the lessons and wisdom gained from what has ended. I titled a chapter in one of my books, "There Are No Trains to Yesterday." The only possibility at whatever station you find yourself in life, is boarding the train that is moving into the future.

Orson Wells said, "If you want a happy ending, that depends, of course, on where you stop your story."[177] I am immediately reminded of the famous sermon title, "It's Friday – But Sunday's Coming." If you stop the gospel stories with Friday, it remains one of the darkest in human history. If you stop the story with Sunday, it becomes the most pivotal event in human history and the story that has brought faith, courage, and hope to millions through countless generations. Easter was not just a new day, it

176 Poole, Charles E. *The Tug of Home*, 36.
177 Lamott, Anne. *Hallelujah Anyway*, 95.

was literally a new beginning. Old things indeed had passed away and all things had become new.

The question we keep asking ourselves as we age is, "What new beginning is possible for me at this stage of my life? What new opportunity do I see that now belongs to me? Into what new activity do I feel God might be leading me at this point in my pilgrimage?" I believe there is always something we can discover if we view life as a series of new beginnings. It may be extremely painful to write "The End" on some aspect of our lives, but it is always a sign of courage, hope, and promise to be able to write "And Now For Something Brand New" on the next page of existence.

QUESTIONS FOR REFLECTION, DISCOVERY, AND CONVERSATION

1. Which endings have been most difficult for you? How have you managed them?
2. How have you dealt with the reality that "We cannot live the afternoon of life according to the program of life's morning"?
3. In what ways do you believe the quality of the ending determines to a large degree the quality of a new beginning? And, are these new beginnings often as difficult as the endings?

C
H
A
P
T
E
R
16

LEARN TO LIVE IN THE NOW

SETTING THE STAGE

The average person checks his phone 110 times a day and nearly once every 6 seconds in the evening. Our perpetual byte-size interactions are not only a detriment to our concentration, focus, productivity, and personal safety, but they're also hurting our intelligence. A 2005 study at King's College in London University found that when distracted, workers suffered a ten-to-fifteen-point IQ loss — a greater dumbing down than experienced when smoking marijuana. (Under a major heading, The Age of Distraction).[178]

Malcolm Muggeridge in a book about the work of Mother Teresa of Calcutta, Indian, said what seemed startling about the work of Mother Teresa and her fellow workers among the thousands of Calcutta's wretched, is that she was totally present to every human being. Every baby discarded in a garbage can, every dying person, every leper, every derelict was a human being worthy of her undivided attention.[179]

---

178 Herman, Amy E. *Visual Intelligence*, 16.
179 Clemmons, William B. *Discovering the Depths* (Tafford Publishing: Victoria, BC, 2006), 19.

Fulfillment need not be what's just around the
corner. In the end wisdom lies in finding it in the
imperfect now.[180]

WHERE ELSE CAN WE REALLY LIVE EXCEPT IN THE PRESENT MOMENT?

The answer to this question seems so obvious that you wonder why it would even be asked. A little reflection clears the way to the answer to that question. As we age, two of the great temptations are to spend a considerable amount of time grieving over days that are no more, regretting and feeling guilty about much in the past we would like to change, and worrying about what the future will hold for us and how we will manage to hold things together (usually financially) to face it.

This is the day the Lord has made; let us rejoice and be glad in it (Psalm 118:24, NRSV).[181] This translation has always reminded me of two daily requirements: to recognize each day as a gift from God and to bring to it a spirit of gratitude and appreciation. Psalm 118 opens and closes with the same refrain: *Give thanks to the Lord, for he is good; his love endures forever.* Verse six gives encouragement for whatever your day may bring: *The Lord is with me; I will not be afraid.* Beginning the day with these assurances and affirmations certainly helps to focus on the now instead of attempting to journey back in time or ahead to the future. Psalm 118:6 is not a bad verse to repeat several times during challenging days when we need to be reminded that we are not alone and that trust is always an option that reaps many more benefits than fear.

"You make the conscious choice of living not in the past or future, in each present moment."[182] This is a decision that has to be made at the beginning of each day. That is why a brief period

---

180 Leland, John. *Happiness Is a Choice You Make*, 178.
181 New Revised Standard Version. Copyright 1989 by the National Council of the Churches of Christ in the United States of America.
182 Arrien, Angeles. *The Second Half of Life*, 176.

of devotional reading and prayer in the morning is so necessary; it helps me make that conscious decision. Too many of us believe that things just happen instead of recognizing the choices we have made, the attitudes we have assumed and what effect they have on the texture and even the events of each day. *"Choose you this day"* is the challenge Joshua issued to the people in order to shift them from the role of victims of circumstances to affirmative action participants in their destiny.

IN THE DAILY "ROLL CALL," ARE YOU HONESTLY ABLE TO RESPOND, "PRESENT"?

A teacher, in commenting on the class to which he was lecturing, wrote: "Sit there, masters of the vacant stare, eyes open, looking forward, living elsewhere, being nowhere."[183] When I taught Junior High School, a frequent lament in the faculty lounge was, "Too many of my students who respond 'present' to the roll call, aren't!" Earlier, I mentioned that this has been called "The Age of Distraction." The bombardment of the many things that call for our attention can easily pull us away from where we are and the persons who are right in front of us.

Mother Teresa's ability (choice, commitment, discipline) to be totally present to every human being (see quote at beginning of chapter) is something most of us envy but would never dream of being able to achieve. I would like to tell you how easily this comes for me but I have always been a person who can easily be "pre-occupied" or whose thoughts easily go off in a dozen directions from where they should be at moment. I really have to work on being totally present and it remains a challenge to this day. But I continue to work on it.

Daniel Simons has done extensive investigation in what he terms "sustained inattentional blindness." The tests involve having participants look at pictures and then tell him what they see. The most obvious example of the "sustained inattentional blindness" is

---

183 Willimon, William H. *Sinning Like a Christian*, 88.

when, after concentrating on a wheat field and telling what they see, he asks, "Did you see the gorilla?"[184] How could anybody miss seeing a gorilla? I couldn't believe such inattention! Then I recalled how many times my wife has asked me, "Did you see that?' and I have to ask, "Did I see what?" Now all I have to do is tell her I'm suffering from "sustained inattentional blindness," even though I don't think she would buy it. And she shouldn't! I simply need to work on being more attentive.

I do know by personal experience that Donald Altman is correct when he maintains: "People are most happy when they are fully *participating* in the moment."[185] But I believe there is a necessary ingredient in that full participation.

We All Need *Enthoozymoozy* Each Day!

> Elliot Engle: Dickens often bemoaned that the very word enthusiasm with its complex Greek derivation did not sound nearly exciting enough to represent such a thrilling, fervent emotion. So he invented a new and much more onomatopoeic term for it: enthoozymoozy. May you catch a severe case of literary enthoozymoozy within these chapters.[186]

My prayer for you would be: May you catch a severe case of enthoozymoozy as you begin each day. And, if someone asks you why you are in such a good mood, it would be a great conversation starter to tell them you have just come down with enthoozymoozy! We have seen *Carpe Deim* often enough to believe that we ought to "seize the day." This is a call to seize the day with extra enthusiasm because it truly is the day given to us to live our fullest in each moment that comes our way. Even if those moments are full of difficulties and challenges. "*Singing in the Rain*" is one of my favorite movies for many reasons. Not the least is the assertion that we

---

184 Peterson, Jordan B. *12 Rules for Life,* 96.
185 Altman, Donald. *Clearing Emotional Clutter,* 9.
186 Engel, Elliot. *A Dab of Dickens & A Touch of Twain* (New York: Pocket Books, 2002), xvii.

can sing and dance in the rain, if we decide to do so. Anybody can sing in the sunshine but to learn to sing in the rain is to learn how to refuse to let circumstances determine how you respond to life.

"The neurologist Oliver Sacks, on learning that he had terminal cancer of the liver, wrote that the nearness of death gave him a sudden clear focus, and no patience for anything nonessential."[187] One of the gifts of our later years ought to be that we no longer worry and fret about things that really don't matter. When I look back on my life, I am appalled at the many things over which I fumed and stewed. Most of them now seem so small and of little consequence. At most, they were just irritating and bothersome. Surely we don't have to wait until our situation is like that of Oliver Sacks to decide that we are no longer going to waste time on anything nonessential. Each day we ought to ask, "What is really important in my life? What really matters? What really counts?" These are the things that ought to be our focus.

One person wrote about Pierre Teilhard de Chardin: "He was alive to everything there is to alive to and in the right ways."[188] Unwrapping that idea has to be done by each of us at the beginning of each day. It calls for discernment and decision because not everything is worth that investment.

IN ORDER TO LIVE A LOT WE HAVE TO GIVE A LOT

Gratitude and generosity are usually two hallmarks of those who find their senior years enriching and satisfying. Although cited in an earlier chapter, John Wesley's famous "sermon" continues to be the formula for the truly good life:

> Do all the good you can,
> By all the means you can,
> In all the ways you can,
> In all the places you can,

---

187 Leland, John. *Happiness is a Choice*, 211.
188 Elie, Paul. *The Life You Save May Be Your Own* (New York: Farrar, Straus and Giroux, 2003), 322.

To all the people you can,
As long as ever you can. [189]

Regardless of how limited our resources, we can always go about doing good. Most of us will never be able to do the spectacular goodness that makes headlines or make contributions that have a huge impact on our culture. Mother Teresa's poem "The Drops of Love" clearly describes what each of us *can* do:

Do not think that love, in order to be genuine,
has to be extraordinary.
What we need is to love without getting tired.
How does a lamp burn?
Through the continuous input of small drops of oil.
If the drops of oil run out,
the light of the lamp will cease,
and the bridegroom will say, "I do not know you."
(Matthew 25:12)

My daughters, what are these drops of oil
in our lamps?
They are the small things of daily life:
faithfulness,
punctuality,
small words of kindness,
a thought for others,
our way of being silent,
of looking, of speaking,
and of acting.

These are the true drops of love.
Be faithful in small things because it is in them
that your strength lies. [190]

---

189 Peck, M. Scott. *An Anthology of Wisdom*, 264.
190 Altman, Donald, *Clearing Emotional Clutter*, 133-134

As we get older, the small things become more important in our lives. I think we begin to realize how important these small things are in everybody's life. It is amazing how a grateful word to the baggers at the grocery store can often bring a smile to someone who probably doesn't hear that very often. One resident of an assisted-care facility made it a practice to find specific ways to say "thank you" to the people who cleaned the room, changed the sheets on her bed, brought her medications, gave her therapy, and ministered to her in any way. She told me she was genuinely grateful for the excellent care she received and she let the daily room cleaner know how much better she felt to be in a "spic and span" place to live.

Eleanor Roosevelt said at seventy-four, "When you cease to make a contribution, you begin to die."[168] That means any contribution you are able to make, regardless of its size. Our strength does lie in the small things that we are able to do when life puts limitations and restrictions on our abilities

I couldn't help but think of certain people I have known through the years when I read this piece of wisdom from Frederick L. Collins: "Always remember there are two types of people in this world. Those who come into a room and say, 'Well, here I am!' and those who come in and say, 'Ah, there you are!'"[191] I immediately thought of one of the true saints I have known, Wayne Oates. He never said, "There you are," but that is what you felt whenever you had a conversation with him. He made you feel as though you were the most important person in the world! The founder of the pastoral care movement, the author of over fifty books, a respected counselor, and much sought after speaker, he never made you feel as though you were intruding on his time. He made you feel as though it was his privilege to have this time with you.

For some reason, the gospel writers did not see fit to include it. It is only in the book of Acts that we find this saying of Jesus: *It is more blessed to give than to receive* (Acts 20:35). It is easy to think how blessed the other person is to receive, but it becomes

---

191 Peck, M. Scott. *An Anthology of Wisdom*, 116.

ever more true that it is in the giving that we feel truly blessed. It is not a bad way to begin the day with the question, "What can I give today that will be a blessing to someone?" If the day begins that way, when the day is over, we are usually able to pray, "Thank you, Lord, for allowing me to give something this day to someone who needed what I gave. Thank you for giving me the blessing I needed in order to let me know you still have a place and purpose for me in your world."

QUESTIONS FOR REFLECTION, DISCOVERY, AND CONVERSATION

1. How difficult is it for you to be fully present where you are? How have you attempted to do this more effectively?
2. In what ways have you attempted to put *enthoozymoozy* into your life?
3. Do you believe that in order to live a lot we have to give a lot? In what ways have you been able to do this?

Bringing It All Together

The Four Overarching Themes of the Book

Facing the Realities of Aging

I can think of no more striking illustration of the consequences of ignoring reality than the tragic story of the Titanic. A recent find is *How It Happened: TITANIC*, edited by Geoff Tibballs. The book consists entirely of survivor's tales and contemporaneous newspaper reports from both sides of the Atlantic. The jacket reads: "Here are eyewitness accounts full of details that range from poignant to tragic and even humorous, stage by stage, from the Titanic's glorious launch in Belfast to the somber sea burial services of those who perished on her first and only voyage."[192]

Accounts written by others have been stirring, but nothing takes the place of listening to those who were aboard the ship on the fateful night of April 14, 1912.

> Mrs. Frank M Warren of Portland, Oregon, lost her husband when the Titanic went down. She remarked how, immediately after the collision, someone had handed her a piece of ice as a souvenir….Mr. Warren told her there was absolutely no danger and that with her watertight compartments the vessel could not possibly sink and that in all probability the only effect of the accident would be the delaying of the arrival in New York three or four days.[193]

The assumption shared by almost everyone on board was that the ship was unsinkable. This illusion may have led to such carelessness as: failing to provide the lookouts (watching for icebergs)

192 Tibballs, Geoff. *How It Happened: TITANIC* (London: Robinson, 2018)
193 Ibid, 53.

with glasses, failure to decrease speed in areas known to be infested with icebergs, failure to hold any disaster drills for the passengers and crew, failure to utilize the full capacity of the available lifeboats (only 706 persons were saved in boats designed to hold 1,176),and the inexcusable failure to provide a sufficient number of lifeboats for the entire number of persons on board (the ship had only sixteen instead of the necessary forty-eight). Of course, if the ship was unsinkable, why would you need lifeboats?

This is why I chose to begin this book on how we handle aging with the plea to remain enrolled in one of life's on-going courses, "Reality 101." We shake our heads at the unpreparedness that doomed this ship on its maiden voyage. Although I will not compare my observations and suggestions with the recommendations from the official inquiries undertaken by the United States Senate which began on April 19, 1912, I have attempted to shatter some of the illusions that keep us from facing life's realities – especially in the senior years. The Titanic's sinking was not inevitable. So much could and should have been done since it was known the voyage lay through waters that contained huge chunks of ice. There is so much we can and should do because we know that our later years are full of chunks of incapacity and potential destruction. We are not invincible. We are vulnerable. But there is so much we can do to make this a much more pleasant and satisfying voyage. It all begins with cooperating with an oft repeated slogan on a sitcom: "These are the conditions that prevail."

ASSUMING PERSONAL PRO-ACTIVE RESPONSIBILITY

After facing the reality of any situation, the next question is, "What am *I* going to do about this?" This may involve receiving good advice from friends or counseling or extended research – and, always, prayer and meditation. But the key is our willingness to be proactive in whatever life offers. Learning to live with increasing losses and limitations, practicing the daily routines that are essential to good physical and emotional health, learning to negotiate well the endings and beginnings – all of these begin with our assuming responsibility and being willing to do the hard work necessary for the achievement of each.

Two quotes speak to often neglected aspects of what assuming that responsibility means. [194]

> Our success is less dependent on IQ than on grit, curiosity, and persistence. The essential ingredient is encountering adversity in childhood and learning to overcome it.
>
> When Michelangelo finally completed painting over 400 life size figures on the ceiling of the Sistine Chapel, he is reported to have written, "If people knew how hard I worked to get my mastery, it wouldn't seem so wonderful after all."

Aging is not something you begin to work on when you reach seventy. If you wait until then, everything becomes more difficult. The better the decisions, attitudes, and habits we develop along the way, the easier we will find the negotiations into the challenging senior years.

The book, *Making It Stick,* (which is about life-long learning) has a big reminder for those of us who get too easily discouraged at our progress. The chapter *Failure and the Myth of Errorless Learning,* is most encouraging:

> This is the belief that errors by learners are counterproductive.
>
> People who are taught that learning is a struggle that often involves making errors will go on to exhibit a greater propensity to tackle tough challenges and will tend to see mistakes not as failures but as lessons and turning points along the past to mastery.
>
> Effort and learning change the brain.[195]

My reason for writing my last book, *All I Need to Know I'm Still Learning at 80,* was the recognition that perfection is not possible

---

194 Brown, Pater C., Henry L. Roediger III, & Mark A. McDonald, *Make It Stick.* (Cambridge: The Belknap Press, 2014), 182, 184.
195 Ibid., 90-92.

and mistakes and miss-steps are inevitable. However, they are *my* mistakes and *my* miss-steps because I am responsible for my life and I'm still a learner.

RECOGNIZING THE POWER OF PERSPECTIVE AND ATTITUDE

Being aware of the greatest freedom I *always* have, regardless of the circumstances, is a life-changing recognition. It saves us from being the "victim" and places us in the role of "chooser." This does not make it automatic or easy. It calls for increasing courage and wisdom as the years lengthen.

> You could falsely assume that joy is something that simply "happens" in life or something you just stumble upon. But joy is often the result of specific choices and can flow from the way you lead your life. That is, joy is often the results of your actions.[196]

I am impressed by the way this quote ties wisdom and faith together. I am impressed by the way it ties our choices and actions together as the road to joy. "I'm just waiting for the joy bug to bite me," is not exactly what anyone ever said to me, but that was the essence of their waiting for joy to overpower them in some way.

In seeking to become the unique persons we believe God has called us to be, attitude, perspective, and actions all work together. (They certainly cannot work separately). Henri Nouwen, another of my favorite writers, provides these encouraging and challenging words:

> Often we want to be somewhere other than where we are, or even to be someone other than who we are. We tend to compare ourselves constantly with others and wonder why we are not as rich, as intelligent, as simple, as generous, or as saintly as they are. Such comparisons make us feel guilty, ashamed, or jealous. It is very important to realize that our vocation is hidden in where we are and who we are. We are unique human beings, each with a call to realize in life what

---

196 Martin, James. *Between Heaven and Mirth*, 120.

nobody else can, and to realize it in the concrete context of the here and now.

We will never find our vocations by trying to figure out whether we're better or worse than others. We are good enough to do what we are called to do. Be yourself![197]

Keeping Faith and Hope 📖 Alive and Well

I simply cannot imagine what life would be like (especially in my eighties) without the faith and hope that beyond this life there is certainly more. Even though I recognize death as the great mystery and acknowledge how little we are told about the next life, I continue to have a "resurrection faith." If Friday had finished the life and ministry of Jesus, it would have marked the end of an outstanding career of teaching and healing. No one expected a resurrection. Sunday morning found the disciples in hiding for fear that the authorities would arrest them for being followers of the Nazarene. Only some women had the courage to go to the grave (a cave with a huge stone rolled in front of it) with spices to anoint the dead body. The only question they had was, "Who will roll away the stone so that we can enter the tomb."

When they arrived, they found the entrance open, and upon entering heard the most unbelievable words ever uttered in human history: "Jesus is not here. He has been raised from the dead. Tell his disciples that he plans to meet them in Galilee." According to the Gospel of Mark (the earliest of the gospels), the reaction of the women was just as you might expect: *Trembling and bewildered, the women went out and fled from the tomb. They said nothing to anyone because they were afraid.* " And according to the earliest manuscripts and most reliable scholars, this is the original ending of Mark.

I have no proof that anything like this ever happened except for the continued witness of almost 2,000 years from those who passed down the story they had heard from those who were ac-

---

197 Nouwen, Henri J. M. *Bread for the Journey.* (New York: HarperOne, 1997)

tual witnesses to the event. The message was simple: "We have seen him. He is alive!" Nothing short of this miracle could have brought the kind of change we witness in the disciples as described in the book of Acts. It was so revolutionary an event that the day of worship changed from Saturday to Sunday. (Remember: all the original Christians were Jewish and the Christian movement remained a part of Judaism for a number of years.)

Why can't we logically make room for such an event as the resurrection in this kind of a universe? We have hinted at its immensity, but here is another way to describe it (with a little humorous twist at the end):

> Now the edge of the universe is roughly ninety billion trillion miles away (roughly being the word you use when your estimate could be off by a million miles), the visible universe is a million million million million miles across, and all the galaxies in the universe are moving away from all the other galaxies in the universe at the same time.
>
> This is called galactic dispersal, and may explain why some children have a hard time sitting still.
>
> And then there's all that we don't know. A staggering 96 percent of the universe is made up of black holes, dark matter, and dark energy. These mysterious, hard to see, and even harder to understand phenomena are a major engine of life in the universe, leaving us with 4 percent that is actually knowable.[198]

No one can persuade me that resurrection is not possible in a universe that is so miraculous that it takes my breath away. To think that only 4 percent is knowable to us leaves a lot of room for God to do just about anything we can or cannot imagine.

We are way too complex,
and so is the world –
too much surprise,
too many possibilities,
too much that defies our limited logical categories –

---

198 Bell, Rob. *What We Talk About When We Talk About God.* (New York: HarperOne, 2014), 24, 27.

> *to fit everything through the narrow filter of*
> *reason alone.*[199]

I usually don't like to string quotes together, but I will do it here because they speak so clearly and directly to things that will keep our faith and hope alive and well.

> *From "The Lion in Winter": There's one memorable line where the sharp-tongued Eleanor of Aquitaine (Katherine Hepburn) says to King Henry (Peter O'Toole): "In a world where carpenters are resurrected, anything is possible!" That in a nutshell is the truth of Easter.*[200]

> *(In a discussion on the circus and the famous trapeze act with the flyer and the catcher): "Dying," Nouwen reflected, "is trusting the catcher."*[201]

> *When John Quincy Adams was eighty years old, he was asked by a friend, "How is Mr. Adams today?" The former president is reported to have replied, "He is quite well, thank you, but the house in which he lives is becoming a little dilapidated; in fact, almost uninhabitable. I think John Adams will have to move out before long. But he, himself, is well, thank you, quite well."*[202]

> *Dr. Bernie Siegal: "On my father-in-law's headstone it reads: 'He Just Fell Up.'"*[203]

These affirmations of faith and hope certainly provide the inspiration and motivation to live fully in the now of each day and

---

199 Ibid., 70.

200 Cartwright, David R. *Wounded by Truth, Healed by Love.* (Gonzalez, FL: Energion Publications, 2014).

201 Ellsberg, Robert. *The Saints guide to Happiness.* (New York: North Point Press, 2003).

202 Seymour, Robert C. *Aging Without Apology,* 100-101.

203 Scott, Williard. *The Older the Fiddle, the Better the Tune,* 114.

fulfill the well-known declaration of Irenaeus: "The glory of God is a human being fully alive."

It comes as no surprise to me that the last word in the Bible is "Amen!" I'm just surprised it doesn't end with: "Amen! Amen! Amen! and Amen!"

A Big Addendum

The Necessity of On-Going Forgiveness

Most of us in the Christian tradition pray what is commonly called "The Lord's Prayer" (but technically is "The Disciples' Prayer") at least once a week. If you follow a devotional guide as I do, it is prayed every day. So each of my days is begun praying, *Forgive us our trespasses as we forgive those who trespass against us.* Another possible valid (and disturbing!) translation is: *Forgive us our trespasses in proportion as we have forgiven those who trespass against us.* This prayer that Jesus taught us to pray is the recognition that forgiveness is an on-going necessity in our lives. Likewise, forgiving others is an ongoing necessity. It is the daily reminder of just how much we depend on the grace of God for our daily existence and for the maintenance of all our relationships.

Brennan Manning's testimony in *All is Grace* is: "But if I've learned anything about the world of grace, it's that failure is always a chance for a do-over."[204] Many have been shocked by this, Manning's last book, because in it he confesses his on-going battle with alcoholism. The book begins with some reader testimonies, including this one:

> Initially I was confused, wondering how Brennan could preach a powerful message of grace but live a powerless life of chronic alcoholism.
>
> I learned the truth of the gospel from Brennan, the same gospel you will find in this book: that in the end, my sin will never outweigh God's grace.[205]

A part of a poem by Manning, could well be the conclusion of his book:

---

204 Manning, Brennan. *All is Grace,* 162.
205 Ibid., 19.

> *Now a prodigal I'll always be*
> *yet still my Father runs to me.*
> *All is grace.*[206]

I bought the book because of the title, *Friends Divided: John Adams and Thomas Jefferson* and the endorsement on the front cover: "Magisterial…Recounts not only the lives of these two greatest founders but also the creation of the republic." Gordon S. Wood does not disappoint on one page of this delightful and informative read. It illuminated the pages of this early period in our nation's history like nothing I have ever read. It is another of my must read recommendations.[207]

In the midst of the turmoil and chaos of public political life (I'm referring to then and not just now), these two giants of history formed a deep friendship that was fractured by acrimonious writings about their many conflicting points of view. For eleven years the two had no contact with one another.

Their story of forgiveness and reconciliation is a teaching model for just how challenging such reconciliation is. "I'm sorry," simply won't cut it in most situations. We have the invaluable legacy of the 158 letters the two wrote to each other over a period of fourteen years. (I wonder what sort of legacy the current tweets will provide future generations? I'll save this for another rant!) Forgiveness and reconciliation came slowly and not without the help and prodding of a friend Benjamin Rush.

Most are familiar with the famous line that Adams sent to Jefferson: "You and I ought not to die before we have explained ourselves to each other." That was attempted in the 158 letters the two exchanged (all written with pen and ink).

Forgiveness begins with our efforts to understand ourselves as well as the other person. And it takes time. "I forgive you," is frequently uttered much too quickly and old resentments lie

---

206 Ibid., 70.
207 Wood, Gordon S. *Friends Divided.* New York: Penguin Books, 2017.
    The information in the following paragraphs comes from the chapter "Reconciliation," pages 356-388.

dormant only to resurface at a season when they are once again needed as ammunition.

Both died, only a few hours apart, on July 4, 1826, the fiftieth anniversary of the signing of the Declaration of Independence.

> "There is no question that the emotional bond between the two patriarchs was restored and the friendship recovered toward the end...But the more mundane truth is that they never faced and therefore never fully resolved all their political differences; they simply outlived them."[208]

As has often been said, "All our disagreements may not be resolved, but we can agree to disagree." What can be more important than keeping relationships alive and well through on-going forgiveness. It is no small thing that Paul was convinced that he had been called to the ministry of reconciliation and that same calling belongs to us. Such a much needed ministry can easily be claimed by those of us who are senior adults and we'll never find a shortage of occasions on which to exercise it.

---

208 Ellis, Joseph J. *Founding Brothers*. New York: Vintage Books, 2000), 244.

Bibliography of Quoted Sources

Alda, Alan. *Things I Overheard While Talking to Myself.* New York: Random House Trade Paperbacks, 2008.

Altma, Donald. *Clearing Emotional Clutter.* New York: MJF Books, 2016.

Alzheimer's Disease Research. *A BrightFocus Foundation Program.* Clarksburg, MD, 2018.

Arrien, Angeles. *The Second Half of Life.* Boulder: Sounds True, 2005.

Bailey, John. *Iris and the Friends.* London: Duckworth, 1999.

_____. *Elegy for Iris.* New York: St. Martin's Press, 1999.

Bell, Rob. What We Talk About When We Talk About God. New York: HarperOne, 2014.

Bridges, William. *Transitions: Making Sense of Life's Changes.* Reading, MA: Addison-Wesley Publishing Company, 1980.

Brokaw, Tom. *A Lucky Life Interrupted.* New York: Random House, 2016.

Brown, Guy. *The Living End.* London: Macmillan, 2008.

Brown, Peter C.; Roediger III, Henry L.; and McDaniel, Mark A. *Make It Stick.* Cambridge: The Belknap Press, 2014.

Broyles, Stephen E. *The Wind That Destroys and Heals.* Colorado Springs: Shaw Books, 2003.

Buford, Bob. *Half Time.* Grand Rapids: Zondervan, 2008.

Cartwright, David. *Wounded by Truth, Healed by Love.* Gonzalez, FL: Energion Publications, 2014.

Chopra, Deepak. *Ageless Body, Timeless Mind.* New York: Harmony Books, 1993.

Chittister, Joan. *The Gift of Years.* New York: BlueBrtidge, 2008.

Clemmons, William B. *Discovering the Depths.* Tafford Publishing: Victoria, BC, 2006.

Cloud, Henry. *Never Go Back.* New York: Howard Books, 2014.

Costco Connection, The. May, 2017.

Creagan, Edward T., ed. *Mayo Clinic on Healthy Aging.* Rochester: Mayo Clinic, 2001.

Domina, Lynn, ed. *Poets on the Psalms.* San Antonia: Trinity University Press, 2008.

Elie, Paul. *The Life You Save May Be Your Own.* New York: Farrar, Straus and Giroux, 2003.

Ellis, Joseph J. *Founding Brothers.* New York: Vintage Books, 2000.

Ellsberg, Robert. *The Saints' Guide to Happiness.* New York: North Point Press, 2003.

Engel, Elliot. *A Dab of Dickens & A Touch of Twain.* New York: Pocket Books, 2002.

Evans, Harold. *Do I Make Myself Clear?* New York: Little, Brown, and Company, 2017.

Eyre, Richard. *Spiritual Serendipity.* New York: Simon & Schuster, 1997.

Finkelstein, Michael. *77 Questions for Skillful Living.* New York: William Morrow, 2013.

Fischer, Kathleen. *Imaging Life After Death.* New York; Paulist Press, 2004.

Flynt, Wayne. *Keeping the Faith.* Tuscaloosa: The University of Alabama Press, 2011.

Fox, Michael J. *A Funny Thing Happened On the Way to the Future.* New York: Hyperion, 2003.

Frankl, Victor. *Man's Search for Meaning.* Boston: Beacon Press, 1959.

Fries, James F. and Crapo, Lawrence M. *Vitality and Aging.* San Francisco: W. H. Freeman and Company, 1981.

Gawande, Atul. *Being Mortal.* New York; Metropolitan Books, 2014.

Grietens, Eric. *Resilience.* Boston: Mariner Books, 2015.

Graham, Billy. *Nearing Home.* Nashville: Thomas Nelson, 2011.

Grant, Adam. *Originals: How Non-Conformists Move the World.* New York: Viking, 2016.

Hansen, Brant. *Blessed Are the Misfits.* Nashville: W. Publishing, 2017.

Heath, Chip and Heath, Dan. *Switch.* New York: Broadman Books, 2010.

Herman, Amy E. *Visual Intelligence.* Boston: An Eamon Dolan Book, 2016.

Hunsinger, Deborah Van. *Bearing the Unbearable.* Grand Rapids: William B. Eerdmans, 2015.

King, Maxwell. *The Good Neighbor.* New York: Abrams Press, 2018.

Kreamer, Anne. *It's Always Something.* New York: Random House, 2011.

Kuhn, Clifford. *It All Starts With a Smile.* Louisville: Butler Books, 2007.

_____. *The Fun Factor.* Louisville: Minerva Books, 2002.

Kung, Hans. *The Christian Challenge.* Garden City: Doubleday, 1979.

Lama, The Dala; Tutu, Desmond; and Abrams, Douglas. *The Book of Joy.* New York: Avery, 2016.

Lamott, Anne. *Hallelujah Anyway.* New York: Riverhead Books, 2017.

Leland, John. *Happiness is a Choice You Make.* New York: Sarah Crichton Books, 2018.

Manning, Brennan. *All is Grace.* Colorado Springs: David C. Cook, 2011.

McGraw, Phillip C. *Life Strategies.* New York: Hyperion, 1999.

McHugh, Adam S. *Introverts in the Church.* Downers Grove, IL: IVP Books, 2009.

Martin, James. *Between Heaven and Mirth.* New York: HarperOne, 2011.

_____. *The Jesuit Guide to Almost Everything.* New York: HarperOne, 2010.

Mayne, Michael. *Learning to Dance.* London: Darton, Longman and Todd, 2001.

Mitteldorf, Josh and Sagan, Dorion. *Cracking the Code.* New York: Flatiron Books, 2016.

Morris, Jonathan. *The Way to Serenity.* New York: HarperCollins, 2014.

Nouwen, Henri J. M. *Bread for the Journey.* New York: HarperOne, 1997.

Nye, Bill. *Everything All At Once.* New York: Rodale, 2017.

O'Brien, Mary. *Successful Aging.* Concord, CA: Biomed General, 2005.

Ortberg, John. *God is Closer Than You Think.* Grand Rapids: Zondervan, 2005.

_____. *Who is This Man?* Grand Rapids: Zondervan, 2012.

Peck, M. Scott. *An Anthology of Wisdom*. Kansas City: Ariel Books, 1996.

_____with Von Waldner, Marilyn. *Gifts for the Journey*. New York: HarperSanFrancisco, 1995.

Peterson, Eugene. *The Message*. Colorado Springs: Navpress, 2002.

Peterson, Jordan B. *12 Rules for Life*. Toronto: Random House Canada, 2018.

Poole, Charles E. *The Tug of Home*. Macon: Peake Road, 1997.

Postman, Neil. *Amusing Ourselves to Death*. New York: Penguin Books, 2005.

Prather, Hugh. *The Little Book of Letting Go*. New York: MJF Books, 2000.

Rohr, Richard and Morrell, Mike. *The Divine Dance*. New Kensington, PA: Whitaker House, 2016.

_____. *Grace in Action*. New York: Crossroad Publishing Company, 1994.

_____with Feister, Jon Bookser. *Hope Against Darkness*. Cincinnati: St. Anthony Messenger Press, 2001.

_____. *Soul Brothers*. Maryknoll, NY: Orbis Books, 2004.

Schofield, Stephen, ed. *In Search of C.S. Lewis*. South Plainfield, NJ: Bridge Publishing, Inc. 1983.

Scott, Williard. *The Older the Fiddle, the Better the Tune*. New York: Hyperion, 2003.

Seymour, Robert E. *Aging Without Apology*. Valley Forge: Judson Press, 1995.

Shanks, Lela Knox. *Your Name is Hughes Hannibal Shanks*. Lincoln, NE: University of Nebraska Press, 1996.

Shideler, Mary McDermott. *In Search of the Spirit*. New York: Ballantine Books, 1985.

Smith, Huston. *And Live Rejoicing.* Novata: New World Library, 2012.

Steinke, Peter. *Teaching Fish to Walk.* Austin: New Vision Press, 2016.

Strawn, Brent A. *The Old Testament is Dying.* Grand Rapids: Baker Academic, 2017.

Sweet, Leonard. *Soul Salsa.* Grand Rapids: Zondervan, 2000.

Taylor, John V. *The Easter God.* New York: Continuum, 2003.

Tengbom, Mildred. *Moving Into a New Now.* Minneapolis: Augsburg, 1997.

Teresa, Mother. *In the Heart of the World.* Novato, CA: New World Library, 1999.

Tickle, Phyllis. *The Divine Hours.* New York: Doubleday, 2001.

Turner, Matthew Paul. *The Christian Culture.* Lake Mary, FL: Relevant Books, 2004.

Valliant, George E. *Aging Well.* Boston: Little Brown and Company, 2001.

Walsch, Neal Donald. *When Everything Changes Change Everything.* Ashland, OR: EmNin Books, 2009.

Ward, Geoffrey C. *American Originals.* New York: HarperCollins, 1991.

Webb, Lance. *Conquering the Seven Deadly Sins.* New York: Abingdon Press, 1995.

Wells, David F. *The Courage to Be Protestant.* Grand Rapids: Willaim B. Eerdmans, 2008.

Wicks, Robert. *No Problem.* Notre Dame: Sorin Books, 2014.

Wiesel. Elie. *From the Kingdom of Memory. New York: Schocken Books, 1990.*

Wilkes, Paul. *Beyond the Walls.* New York: Image Books, 1999.

Willimon, William H. *Sinning Like a Christian*. Nashville: Abing-
  don, 2005.
Wolfelt, Alan D. and Duvall, Kirby J. *Healing Your Grief About
  Aging*. Fort Collins, CO: Companion Press, 2012.

CPSIA information can be obtained
at www.ICGtesting.com
Printed in the USA
FFHW021703110819
54191266-59941FF